IN SEARCH OF...

THE *Real*
Spirit
OF *Christmas*

Discovery House Publishers

Books, music, and videos that feed the soul with the Word of God

Box 3566 Grand Rapids, MI 49501

IN SEARCH OF...

THE *Real* *Spirit* OF *Christmas*

DAN SCHAEFFER

Discovery House Publishers is affiliated with RBC Ministries,
Grand Rapids, Michigan 49512.

Discovery House books are distributed to the trade exclusively by
Barbour Publishing, Inc., Uhrichsville, Ohio.

"The Angels' Point of View" from *New Testament Christianity*
by J. B. Phillips is used by permission of Mrs. Vera Phillips
and the Phillips estate.

Unless otherwise noted, Scripture quotations are from The New
International Version (NIV), © 1973, 1978, 1984 by the
International Bible Society. Used by permission of Zondervan Bible
Publishers.

Interior design by Sherri L. Hoffman

Library of Congress Cataloging-in-Publication Data
Schaeffer, Daniel, 1958 –
    In search of—the real spirit of Christmas / by Dan Schaeffer
        p. cm.
    Includes bibliographal references.
        ISBN: 1-57293-106-X
    1. Christmas.   I. Title.
BV45.S325 2003
263'.915—dc21   2003010555

Printed in Italy
05 06 07 08 09 / PBI / 10 9 8 7 6 5 4

*For those who have longed to experience
the real Christmas spirit*

❄

No one truly writes a book alone. While I had the germ of an idea for a book, it took the publishing eye of an expert, Carol Holquist, to see its potential, encouragement by Tim Gustafson, expert editing by Judith Markham, and much behind-the-scenes work by the rest of the faithful staff at Discovery House Publishing. I was also given the gift of patience and encouragement from my wife and family. To all who helped me, and model so beautifully what this book is about, I thank you from the bottom of my heart and wish you a truly Merry Christmas!

Table of Contents

Introduction

*E*ach year, millions of people go in search of the real spirit of Christmas. True, some want to find it only so they can try to package it and sell it. But others gaze at the Christmas tree, the presents, and all the decorations and wonder: *What is all this really about?* Sure, we know the *story* of Christmas, but what is the *spirit* of Christmas we hear so much about. Does it exist? And if so, how can we hope to find it?

In our attempt to isolate the one and only true Christmas spirit, we try to separate fact from fiction. Most of us have a sneaking suspicion that much of our emotional attachment to the season stems more from our Santa Claus days than the news announced to the shepherds some twenty centuries ago. So we read the Christmas story in Matthew and Luke and we parrot all the appropriate clichés: "Jesus is the reason for the season," and "Let's keep the Christ in Christmas." But when all is said and done, we still wonder what fuels our Christmas sentiment. Is what we are feeling the true Christmas spirit or merely the lingering pleasant remnants of "the holidays"?

Let's face it. Family get-togethers, decorating Christmas trees, singing in or listening to Christmas choirs, caroling, candy cane lanes, the wonderful smells of baking Christmas goodies, Christmas Eve traditions, opening gifts around the Christmas tree, and fond memories of Christmases past are powerfully pleasant and warm influences. And to many, this is what passes for the Christmas spirit. But deep inside, many also wonder if there's more to it than that.

How often does the end of an exhausting Christmas season leave us with a sense of regret? We've done it again! We've come to our King's birthday party empty-handed one more time. And so it goes, on and on, as each year we struggle to know how to properly celebrate His marvelous entrance into our world. We know what He did—even those who don't believe it know the story of the first Christmas. But how deeply have we thought about that story and its implications for our lives?

The problem is that when something becomes too familiar to us, we have trouble seeing it in a new way. That is the purpose of this book: to help you see beyond the familiar and find the true spirit of Christmas—the spirit that is meant to decorate our hearts the way lights decorate a barren tree. So join me now in the quest for the real Christmas spirit.

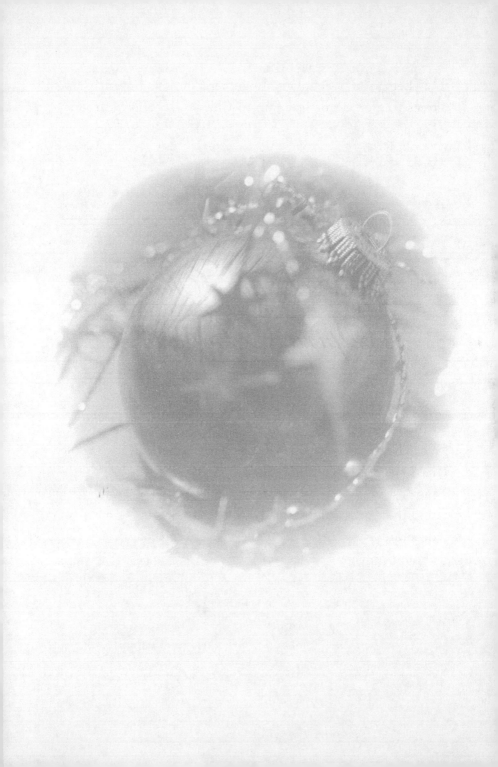

ONE

❄

What Is the Christmas Spirit Anyway?

A Lesson in Catching the Christmas Spirit," read the article headline in our local newspaper. In the piece, the columnist, Bill Johnson, explained that he was engaged in a pilgrimage of the heart, searching for that elusive destination, the true Christmas spirit, and was inviting his readers to join him on his journey. He began in what he felt would be the epicenter of Christmas spirit: a Christmas-tree lot. "Christmas-tree lots, by their very nature, are hotbeds of Christmas spirit," he wrote. "Nobody goes there if they don't have it. So I went to one in Tustin hoping that some would rub off." But, alas, the only people he found there were several mortgage bankers trying to find a tree for their office.[1]

So he decided to visit Santa in the mall. After all, "if he can't get you in the spirit, nobody can." On the way, however, he encountered a festively dressed family and figured they *must* have the Christmas spirit. When he asked them the question, the mother said, "Let's see, yesterday we put up the tree, put the lights on the house, and played all of our Christmas CDs and albums a million times. I'd say we have the Christmas spirit." Sound familiar?

While this family hurried off to buy Christmas earrings that light up, Bill went off to find Santa. When he saw all the children in line, eagerly waiting for their chance to meet the bearded gentleman from the North Pole, Bill thought, *This is what Christmas is about.* But still, something didn't feel right. So he asked the woman at the mall's information desk, "Where might I find the Christmas spirit?"

"It's in your heart," she said, barely glancing up. "It feels warm and glowy, like a mother's love for her child. You can't buy it at any store here, and you can't get it from anybody else. It's in there," she said, pointing to his chest. "It's in your heart."

Conventional wisdom agrees that the Christmas spirit is inside of us somehow, in some way. We just have to find it, or rediscover it. It is a warm and glowy feeling that finally hits us when . . . when . . . ah, there's the rub, isn't it?

Each year as Thanksgiving ushers in the big buildup to Christmas, many seek to outshine and outdazzle their neighbors. More lights, more ornaments, a bigger tree, flashing lights and moving figurines. The more decorations the greater the Christmas spirit, or so it appears. But despite the greatest decorating efforts, many know, deep inside, that there should be more—or less.

The Original Christmas Spirit

As I began writing this book, I decided that if I hoped to discover the real Christmas spirit I would need to reread the real Christmas story. But this time I would pay attention to the reactions of those who first heard of the Christ child's birth. Surely those most closely associated with the first Christmas would display the Christmas spirit.

When I opened my Bible to the gospel of Luke, chapter two, I noticed that the first recorded reaction to Christ's birth was from the shepherds, who "returned, glorifying and praising God for all the things they had heard and seen" (Luke 2:20). This becomes even more remarkable when we understand that shepherds in the first century weren't the pastoral, gentle-eyed, soft-spoken fellows portrayed by Hallmark. They were considered unreliable, untrustworthy, and not a little larcenous. People in "polite society" shunned these uncouth, uncultured, and rough-around-the-edges shepherds. In the first century, shepherds weren't even allowed to testify in a court of law because their truthfulness was so suspect.

Picture a room full of men drinking beer, making disgusting male noises, and cheering on their favorite football teams with gusto and excitement. Add lots of yelling and words that aren't heard in polite society and you come close to describing the crude demeanor of first-century shepherds. So when it says that the shepherds were glorifying and praising God, it does not mean that they were offering artistic praise in highly cultured terms or quiet, reflective praise in articulate phrases. It was more like the last second of a playoff game in overtime, when the home team wins and the whooping and hollering begins. That was the only kind of glorifying they likely knew.

The next reaction we find is that of Simeon, a much different character. "Simeon took him [the Christ child] in his arms, and praised God" (Luke 2:28). Simeon was a quiet, holy man who walked with God, and God had promised that before his death he would see the coming Messiah. His dignified response must have been rich with joy and excitement. He actually held his Lord in his hands. Did tears flow? Did he gaze long upon the child in his arms?

And what of the response of Joseph and Mary? "The child's father and mother marveled at what was said about him" (Luke 2:33). Between the miraculous way in which their baby had been born and the angelic visitations they had already received, it would probably take a lot to amaze these new parents. Yet the more they heard, the more amazed they became. Did Mary and Joseph look at each other and shake their heads in excited bewilderment? Not just their own lives, but also the world itself was being changed, and they were closest to the One who would do the changing.

The rough-around-the-edges shepherds whooping and hollering in the middle of the night, the holy Simeon reverently praising God, and Jesus' own parents showing amazement at what was happening. Everyone's reaction was a little different, according to individual personalities, temperaments, and lifestyles. Everyone responded differently.

A One-Time Event

The more I thought about this, the more I realized that we can never recapture that first Christmas spirit experienced by the eyewitnesses to Christ's birth any more than we can recapture the excitement of our wedding day. Each is a one-time event. If my wife and I revisited our marriage vows each year, it would be a special time, but it would never be quite as special as the first time. There can only be one first time for anything. Every celebration of the event thereafter is simply an anniversary.

What does this mean, then, for this anniversary we celebrate with such fanfare and even hoopla every year? Some people are attracted to Christmas the way they're attracted to a concert or the Super Bowl or the annual Macy's Christmas parade. In the same way, the laughter and fun and good food, theme-decorated trees and miniature lighted villages, the Christmas parties and programs can be contagious. Plus, many do sense that there is a deeper holy meaning to this season, which at least temporarily satisfies their spiritual longing. The shared excitement and anticipation are such wholesome emotions that many are attracted to the celebration of Christmas even when they don't really know what it's all about. But they feel so good about themselves and other people and what they're experiencing that they don't care what it all means. It's like finding relief from the scorching sun. You don't really care what causes the shade; you're just glad it's there.

In other words, many who join the celebration never truly understand it. They are like the people at weddings who laugh louder and drink more than anyone else, and yet are not really close friends to either the bride or groom. They've been invited because they work with the bride or groom or are friends of the couple's parents or have been asked to take pictures or video. But they have no real interest in the two who have just gotten married. Their real interest is in the celebration. Take away the party and you remove their joy. They simply enjoy celebrating, and it doesn't much matter what they celebrate.

This is the essential difference between those who possess the real Christmas spirit and those who don't. If you removed the trees, and the lights, and the poinsettias, and the decorations, and the presents, and the food, and the music, those with the real Christmas spirit would still celebrate.

So if we're going to discover the real Christmas spirit, we must search the Christmas story itself. For many, the Christmas story is warm and quaint and comforting. They associate it with Christmas plays, nativities, and familiar music like "O Little Town of Bethlehem" and "Silent Night." But if you really examine what happened over two thousand years ago, you might begin to scratch your head and say, "What's wrong with this picture?"

Reflection and Celebration

This Christmas, between parties, shopping, and wrapping presents, carve out some quiet time when you can re-read (or perhaps read for the first time) the Christmas story found in Matthew 1:18–2:23 and Luke 1:26–2:40. Because the story is so familiar, you may need to read it in an entirely different manner than you have in the past.

Read slowly and carefully, stopping when necessary to picture the scenes described. As you do, imagine what some of the original characters might have been thinking and feeling as the miraculous events unfolded about them. Try to put yourself in their place.

Imagine how you might have responded to what Mary, Joseph, the shepherds, Simeon, and Anna experienced.

Imagine what it might feel like to be suddenly face to face with an angel or to see one in a dream.

Walk outside at night and try to imagine what the shepherds experienced when the dark sky lit up with the presence of hundreds, perhaps thousands of angels praising God. Would your rejoicing have been loud and boisterous like the shepherds, or would your praise be solemn and quieter like Simeon?

Don't just read the story. Put yourself into it.

TWO

✳

What's Wrong with This Picture?

*T*he debates appear every year like clockwork.

The subject? Public manger scenes. Christians and even other traditionalists want them, while some vocal non-Christians or atheists or ACLU members don't. The editorial pages of newspapers argue back and forth on why we should or shouldn't publicly display nativities. Yet ultimately, somewhere in most communities, we see manger scenes, sometimes even with real people and animals.

Every Christmas, in our living room, we put out our own manger scene—a small, rustic-looking stall, crude but charming, busy with sheep, shepherds, camels, wise men, and two babes in the manger. (The second baby, put there by our youngest child, is from another long-lost set.)

When Dad connects the lights, and Mom adds some appropriate seasonal foliage to cover the top of the stable, it provides all of us a warm, wonderful holiday experience. As I look at our familiar holiday display or those I see on lawns and churches throughout the city, I have to wonder: How could anyone object to this tender, primitive scene of mother and son, hovered over by Joseph and the angels, surrounded by animals and shepherds and a few gaudily painted kings? What's all the fuss about?

The problem is that I've gazed upon the scene so long that I've become numb to it. I've heard the story so often that I've stopped thinking about it. But when I do think about it, I realize that this scene isn't normal. And God doesn't want me to view it as pretty and quaint. He wants me to be appalled at the situation, even bewildered and confused; because when I am, I have to think about the scene rather than ignore it. The manger scene wasn't designed to put me in "the holiday mood." It was intended to shake me to the roots of my soul. Which, by the way, is why each year we have all the fuss and furor about manger scenes. It originates from folks who, while they don't believe a word of the Christmas story, have thought about it enough to be disturbed by its implications. And that's where we all ought to find ourselves: disturbed by the implications.

Christmas is the day we celebrate the entrance of the eternal, omnipotent, omniscient, omnipresent, all-righteous, all-holy, and glorious God into our world. When I stop and consider this fact and then look at that scene of the baby Jesus in the manger, I scratch my head and say, "What's wrong with this picture?"

Four words in this story should challenge my mind, not anesthetize it. "This will be a sign to you: You will find a baby wrapped in cloths and *lying in a manger*" (Luke 2:12, emphasis added). The God of the ages, too glorious to look upon, is lying in a feed trough. The God before whom Moses and Isaiah fell down on their faces, and from whom the cherubim hide their faces, is in a filthy stable. If this story were merely myth, we could smile warmly and safely ignore it. But this isn't myth. It is fact, and at the very least we should find it disturbing.

Lying in a manger. These four familiar, beautiful, magnificent, and glorious words describe far more than the place where baby Jesus was laid. Here is a message from God, a parable in four words, a testament in wood and straw that contains more truth than would fit in a volume of books. In these four words we find the answer to the most pressing questions of life and faith, for there are important reasons why the Christ child had to be found lying in a manger.

A Sign for the Shepherds

*A*t the time of the census decreed by Caesar Augustus, which demanded that all the citizens of the entire Roman Empire had to return to their hometowns to register, Bethlehem must have been swollen with people. Just picture your local mall on the day after Thanksgiving—the busiest shopping day of the year—and multiply that for an entire town. In the midst of congested streets, homes crowded with returning relatives, and inns bursting at the seams, how would a group of shepherds find one child—the child they were seeking? There would have been mothers and babies galore. Which one was the right one?

All the babies were wrapped in some kind of cloths, so that didn't narrow it down. No, the sign for the shepherds was that the baby would be *lying in a manger.* Even in that ancient time and place, a stable for a birthing room and a manger for a crib would have been unusual. This scene *was* strange, and it was intended to be.

Imagine the shepherds entering Bethlehem, eagerly listening in the night for the sounds of a crying baby. Did their search, their inquisitive examination of every shed, draw stares? Did this group of rugged sheepherders, who should have been out in the fields, elicit comments as they moved through the streets? Undaunted, they continued their quest, searching for the promised sign.

And finally their faithfulness was rewarded. They found the promised Savior, Christ the Lord, in the form of "a baby wrapped in cloths and *lying in a manger*." They hadn't gotten the directions wrong. They weren't on a fool's errand. They weren't the victims of some divine practical joke. The shepherds knew without doubt that God had been leading them. The manger was their sign, the heavenly magnet that drew them irresistibly. Without that sign the shepherds had no compass and no hope. The baby in the manger was the Great Shepherd who led these sinful men to a carpenter and his young wife, and, ultimately, to Himself.

The scene was a promised sign to the shepherds, and it was also a billboard for the Christ child's earthly parents.

A Confirmation for Mary and Joseph

*W*hat we celebrate with great joy each year must have been a terrible ordeal for Mary and Joseph. Was this what Mary envisioned when Elizabeth, her friend and relative, had prophesied that she would be blessed and greatly honored among women (Luke 1:42)? Surely she didn't expect a parade, but did she expect this? Mary had great faith, but was it challenged when she entered that stable, heavy with child and exhausted from the long journey?

Somehow I doubt that this young woman—this young girl, probably no more than twelve or thirteen years old—found her circumstances quaint and inspiring. But could she see beyond the dismal scene that greeted her eyes and assaulted her senses? When her labor pains began, with no woman or midwife to help her, when she and Joseph were left alone in a stable to "celebrate" the arrival of the heavenly child, promised them with great miracles and dreams, did she and Joseph ever ask themselves "What's wrong with this picture, God?"

A Bethlehem inn was no Holiday Inn. It was a crude series of stalls built inside an enclosure, with a fire pit for cooking. As dismal as this arrangement was, this was the inn in which there was no room. And despite Mary's obvious pregnancy, no one offered to give up their space for her. So she and Joseph ended up in what was most likely a cave of some sort, where the animals were stabled and where filthy hay and rank animal waste littered the floor.

There, Mary went into labor, crying out in pain and fear, with a beleaguered Joseph her only attendant. It was a carpenter who most likely delivered the Christ child as He came into our world, slippery with blood, His warm body greeted with joltingly cold air. You can't recreate the drama of this scene with a nativity scene, no matter how hard you try.

Yet, after the birth, God sent shepherds to seek out the lonely little family. When the men arrived, they shared their angelic vision and the all-important sign they had been given—a sign to the world—a baby lying in a manger. Not in a palace or an ornately decorated crib befitting the Son of God. Not even in a house, or a room, but outside, in the cold stable. And yet the baby was right where He was supposed to be—lying in a manger. When they saw these rugged worshipers, did Mary and Joseph sigh in relief? Did the joy of realization flood their souls, washing away the debris of doubt that might have begun to accumulate in their hearts?

I think it did, and I think they needed to hear the heavenly pronouncement from the shepherds to know that their present circumstances were holy to God. His plans hadn't gone wrong; His promises hadn't been forgotten. There had been no divine snafus. This was precisely the place God chose to showcase His entrance into our world, wrapped up so tight in swaddling cloths that He couldn't even move.

This grand entrance did not fit His person or His glory. But in it, we begin to see glimmers of His purpose.

No Room for God in the World He Had Made

*A*ctually, it all makes sense. When God returned to His creation, it wasn't *fitting* that bands play, parades march, choirs sing, or heralds trumpet the good news. Because His return *wasn't* good news ... not in this earthly neighborhood. God had long ago been exiled from the hearts and minds of most people. No rulers were willing to step down for Him, no kings were eager to make room for His sovereign kingship. No palaces opened their gates to Him in welcome.

So God entered the world in the one place no one coveted or cared about, a place where no one would fight to keep Him out—a place, in fact, that no one even noticed. The God of the universe spent His first day of humanity lying in a manger, in a cave in Bethlehem.

Yet the eternal God lying helplessly in a manger is an object lesson impossible to ignore. This scene puzzles the critics, and rightly so. It is not uncommon to hear critics of Christianity speak of the wrathful, vengeful, judgmental God of the Old Testament. But would such a God suffer Himself to be disgraced by lying helplessly in a manger? No, the manger scene reveals as much about the mercy and love of God as do any of His words or acts of compassion.

"There was no room for them in the inn." Those familiar words ring out across the centuries. Yet in truth, there was no room for Him anywhere. And this scene, forever frozen in time, reminds us not only of His character but also of ours. The Creator returned to a decidedly hostile world, not with His divine wrath prepared to destroy all that would treat Him with contempt, but in divine mercy prepared to endure all that we could throw at Him. Could God's attitude of mercy and love toward our hostile and rebellious world have been any clearer than when He was found lying in a manger?

When we are having difficulty conjuring up an appropriate Christmas spirit, we need only picture the God of eternity, too glorious for mortal eyes to look upon and live, enduring that filthy and incredibly humiliating setting. It was His love for us that put Him in that manger, though He despised the shame of it. Could He say "I love you" any clearer?

Is there something truly wrong with this picture? If I didn't understand the love of God, I would be forced to laugh out loud. But instead I begin to sense a profound wisdom in this act. For as I picture Him lying in a manger I suddenly see something I'd never have understood otherwise.

So We Could Understand

*I*f the infinite and perfect God had arrived in the company of thousands of angels, too glorious to look upon, descending from heaven in chariots of gold and precious jewels while the angels sang, "Holy, Holy, Holy is our God," He would still have been humbling Himself, but I wouldn't have understood it. I would never have gotten the idea that God was willing to intentionally demean His perfect glory to save someone like me.

In our world, important people tend to associate with other important people; they seek each other out. And being seen with the right people in the right places can take you far. So it is with no little confusion that we view God humbling Himself so drastically before us. Yes, us. You and me. We were the reason He left His glory. We'll never really understand it, not completely anyway. We know what He did, but for the life of us we can't figure out why.

When someone greater than us humbles himself before us in some way, it is a powerful gesture. We are amazed and moved that someone of such stature and status would do such a thing. When someone gives us a gift we don't expect or deserve, we say, "Oh, you shouldn't have." But we are touched by the thought. So when I think about my God in a manger, I shake my head in utter disbelief. But I am so grateful that He did.

God humbled Himself in a way that even a common shepherd would understand, or a child, or a tax-gatherer, or a fisherman, or a fallen woman, or a self-righteous Pharisee, or me. While lying in a manger, God was making an announcement to all who would come to Him. It was a silent message that told us what we desperately needed to know about our God.

Anyone Could Approach Him

*C*ommon folks can't visit the palaces of newborn kings uninvited (and we seldom are). But kings and princes can visit mangers, and so can bakers and weavers, wise men and shopkeepers, priests and children, cattle and sheep. This reality is so simple that it is easy to miss.

The God-Child was announcing in a dramatic way that He had come to be available, to be accessible. He hadn't come to isolate Himself, or to hobnob with only the important people. He had come to mingle with all, to receive them with open arms and put Himself at their disposal. All this He conveyed by simply being found *lying in a manger*!

The ark of the covenant in the Old Testament, with its ornate and precious gold inlaid work of beautiful craftsmanship, housed the Shekinah glory of the Lord. Yet a common feeding trough for beasts of burden hosted the God-Child Himself. "Why?" we ask ourselves. Why indeed! For us! Oh, the wisdom of God. He humbled Himself before us so that we would realize that there was nothing God wouldn't do to bring us back into relationship with Him.

Whenever I am tempted to blurt out, *"Lord, you don't know what it's like to be humiliated like this,"* He points to the manger. When I cry out, *"Lord, I deserve better than this,"* He points to the manger. When I tell God, *"You see all these injustices in my life? Why don't you change them; you have the power,"* He reminds me of the manger. This isn't the stuff of Christmas cards; it is the stuff of transformation.

What's wrong with this picture? Not a thing! Though the manger is disturbing, the message it brings to us is anything but. For this primitive scene of our God *lying in a manger* reminds us of this precious truth: We're no longer alone.

Reflection and Celebration

Inevitably we end up doing a lot of driving or traveling during the Christmas season, with all of our holiday activities, our shopping expeditions, and our visits to friends and family. This year, make the most of your travel time by using it to help you get into the Christmas spirit.

Notice the hospitals you pass in your travels, and each time you pass one, take a few moments to remember how and where your God was born. When I go into a hospital maternity ward or a comfortable home nursery, I think about how bright, clean, healthy, and warm these places are . . . and I marvel anew that my God lay in a manger!

Think about all the doctors, nurses, attendants, expensive equipment, and special medications available to ensure a safe and healthy delivery for today's children. Think of all the conveniences we have that the baby Jesus went without. Think about why God, who could have come in such glory, safety, security, and luxury, decided instead to arrive so humbly.

And every time you see a nativity display, ask yourself: What's wrong with this picture? For those of you who are braver, dare to ask others, "Does this picture make sense to you? Why would the God of the universe enter our world in this manner?" If they don't know, tell them. Tell them.

And finally, if you are feeling humiliated, if you think you deserve more than you have, if you believe life is treating you unjustly—remember the manger! What we suffer involuntarily, He suffered voluntarily. As His suffering had meaning, so does ours. This is the message from the manger!

THREE

❄

No Longer Home Alone

*I*n the popular Christmas movie *Home Alone*, a family plans a European vacation for Christmas. The relatives all arrive for the big event. But in all the commotion the youngest son feels slighted. Expressing his frustration inappropriately, he is punished and sent to a room in the attic. There, in a fit of anger, he wishes that his family would go away so he could be all alone. The next morning, in their rush to get ready and leave for the airport, the family overlooks the little boy in the attic. They get to the airport and board the plane, all the while believing he is with them.

When the little boy wakes, he discovers that there is no one in the house and believes his wish has been granted. He is home alone and he is delighted.

For the next few days, while his family tries frantically to return to him, the little boy has full run of the house. At first he is delirious with joy. He eats all the junk food he wants, watches whatever movie he wants, sleeps wherever he wants, and doesn't have to answer to anyone. But then burglars try to break into the house, and he discovers that his aloneness has made him vulnerable to danger. After the burglars have been foiled with his inventive array of booby traps, the boy realizes how lonely he is. Being alone, without his parents and the rest of his family, isn't as wonderful as he thought it would be. He is sorry he treated them so badly and desperately wants them back again.

When I think about this funny yet poignant movie, I am reminded of humanity's relationship with God. While we lived in the garden with God we were contented; but then we decided we could be even happier if we did not have to answer to Him—if we could do whatever we wanted to do. For awhile we reveled in our newfound freedom. But then we began to feel the emptiness and loneliness that comes from being isolated and alone and at odds with our heavenly Father. In essence, we got homesick.

And that brings me to one of the most common words we hear each and every Christmas: *Immanuel*. The word adorns Christmas cards, is sung in hymns and carols, is painted or sewn on banners, and fills sermon titles. Yet the impact of this word is often lost on us as we overlook or are completely unaware of its true meaning. Immanuel is one of the names of God, one of the most beautiful and enlightening names of God. And it explains one of the great reasons for Christmas in the first place.

Many people do not dwell much on the subject of sin at Christmas. They reserve that for Easter and the story of the crucifixion and the resurrection. Yet we could never get to Easter without Christmas.

Centuries before Christ was born, God promised through the words of Isaiah the prophet: "Therefore the Lord himself will give you a sign: The virgin will be with child and will give birth to a son, and will call him Immanuel" (Isaiah 7:14). Matthew repeats Isaiah's words as he begins to tell the story of the birth of Christ. But the gospel writer goes one step further, telling us what the name *Immanuel* means. "All this took place to fulfill what the Lord had said through the prophet: 'The virgin will be with child and will give birth to a son, and they will call him Immanuel'—*which means, 'God with us'*" (Matthew 1:22–23, emphasis added).

Something more cataclysmic than anything found in the pages of Revelation is here in these three simple words: God with us!

With all our sinfulness and rebellion, we should expect, at best, a holy deity to be finished with us, to wash His hands of us, to cut us off forever—or, at worst, to annihilate us completely. Instead, He bound Himself to us forever by His death on the cross. And He knew this would happen before He came (Matthew 16:21). He committed Himself to be near us for all eternity. This is more than the Christmas story; it is the Christmas miracle.

Furthermore, God didn't simply appear in a cameo role. He actually, physically, lived *among* us for thirty-three years. And rather than cloistering Himself safely away during those years, He approached lepers with a touch, healed the blind with compassion, and fed the hungry with concern. God *with us*. It had always been God over us, God above us, God before us, God on the mountain, God in the temple, God in the cloud. But never before had it been God *with* us.

Author and pastor Leith Anderson writes of an experience he had in Manila that communicates the power of this truth. "Several years ago I was visiting Manila and was taken, of all places, to the Manila garbage dump site. They've constructed shacks out of the things other people have thrown away. And they send their children out early every morning to scavenge for food out of other people's garbage, so they can have family meals. People have been born and grown up there on the garbage dump. They have had their families, their children, their shacks, their garbage to eat, finished out their lives, and died there without ever going anywhere else, even in the city of Manila. It is an astonishing thing.

"But Americans also live on the garbage dump. They are missionaries, Christians who have chosen to leave their own country and communicate the love of Jesus Christ to people who otherwise would never hear it. That is amazing to me. People would leave what we have to go and live on a garbage dump. Amazing, but not as amazing as the journey from heaven to earth. The Son of God made that journey, and He knew what He was doing. He knew where He was going. He knew what the sacrifice would be. He journeyed from heaven to earth on a mission to save the human race."[1]

Imagine our sorrowful destiny if the life of Christ among us had ended with the words, "And God left His creation, which had rejected Him and put Him to death, never to come again." A perfect life, a perfect love, abandoning those who never appreciated it, wanted it, or sought it. Who could blame Him? The thought of such a thing is the stuff of nightmares, not Christmas.

❄

*H*ow blessed we are to live when we do. To have lived during the Old Testament period would have been to cling to the promise, strange to hear and hard to understand, that somehow, at some time, and in some way God would one day be *with us*. Not simply as a remote guiding presence or an awesome spirit filling the temple, but with us personally . . . with *me*!

The glory of Christmas is not a pageant or a play; it is the precious truth that God desired to draw near to His sinful creation, to bind Himself to us irrevocably and forever. It is not a glory we watch; it is one we participate in, one of which we are the focus.

What does this mean for us?

It means we are far more precious to God than we could ever imagine.

I could spend the rest of my life listing why I should be anything but precious to God. When I look at my life honestly and think about God's perfect attributes, I hang my head. I find not one shred of evidence to explain His attitude toward me. Yet Immanuel, God with us, challenges me with the fact that there is something in God so profoundly merciful, gracious, and loving that He desires to be with *me*. That something is not found in me; it is found in Him. But I am the beneficiary. That's why it is called *amazing* grace. The thing I least deserve from Him is the thing He offers to me.

So many things conspire to devalue our existence, and the human choruses here on earth often drown out the heavenly message. Instead of recognizing that God created us and that we're of infinite value, we worry that we're not tall and strong and handsome like the hunk on TV or on the movie screen. We're not sexy and shapely and desirable like the actress or model. We have no extraordinary abilities or gifts or powers that set us apart from the billions of other people on this earth. No one seeks our autograph; no admirers send us cards and letters telling us how wonderful we are—hoping, even dreaming, of catching a glimpse of us. We are not the center of attention everywhere we go. If we're fortunate, we're considered average. We're plain vanilla in a culture that craves the other tantalizing thirty flavors.

Yet the God who came in the form of a babe came so that He could be closer to me—to you! He came to remove the barriers between Him and us. He wants to be *with us*! Whatever humiliation He might have to endure, whatever rejection He might receive, whatever pain He would have to bear would not be too much of a price to pay to be with us forever (Philippians 2:5–8). His expression of perfect love is designed to cast away all our fear.

Why He wants to be with us is too great a mystery to explain. The answer lies in the nature of His merciful, loving being. But *that* He wants to be with us is undeniable.

What does this mean for us?

> ### It means there is far more to celebrate than we thought.

The entrance of God into our world is a cause for great celebration. Yet the manner in which we sought to hasten His exit out of this world certainly causes us to wonder why He would even want to be with us (Acts 2:22–23).

Think of what happens when a marriage that was initially celebrated with a beautiful wedding ceremony and a lavish reception eventually ends in divorce. The wedding pictures, which are no longer a cause of joy or fond memories, are tucked away—sometimes even destroyed—to try and erase painful memories. What began with great hope and joy and love has deteriorated to the point where it is difficult to bear the mention of the other's name. Now, think of our broken relationship with God—what we might term, to use C. S. Lewis's phrase, "the great divorce." In light of that, it would not be surprising if God rejected us. Indeed, we should only be surprised that He didn't.

Yet instead of seeking a divorce, God used our ultimate rejection to cement His relationship with us forever. He did more than just renew His vows with us; He deepened them. He committed to being nearer us than He ever had before, sending His Spirit to dwell within us. And, in a mystery too deep for us, we discover that had been His eternal plan all along. He who is so holy and pure that the cherubim cover their eyes in His presence allowed men of the lowest repute to mock Him and kill Him. How great a love!

That Babe in the manger was God with us, as was that same babe, grown to manhood, hanging on the cross. They were both Immanuel, committed to us for eternity. Who else in your life is that committed to you? Who else would return your unfaithfulness, abandonment, and even apathy with such an act? Who? Only Immanuel! God with us!

What does this mean for us?

It means we will never be alone.

One of the most difficult parts of Christmas for many people is the reality that, culturally, it has become a family time of celebration. For those who live in broken families, who endure fractured, fragile relationships, this only accentuates their pain and aloneness.

For too many, Christmas celebrations are largely lonely affairs. Even those who have many friends can find themselves feeling alone as those friends go off to spend the holidays with their own families. And those who are invited to participate and are welcomed into these gatherings often feel they "do not really belong." They are on the outside looking in, and that is a painful place to be. Christmas, with all its attendant parties and get-togethers, often accentuates our loneliness, our frustration and longing.

In such situations, the Christmas spirit can seem beyond our grasp. But if the real Christmas spirit is connected to something God has done for *us,* then we can still enter into it, even when family ties are weak or severed. For unlike fractured family relationships, Immanuel—God with us—is not isolated from us. Immanuel goes looking for us. He looks in the tenements, the mud huts, the tents, the back alleys, the apartments and condos, the suburbs, the mansions, and everywhere in between.

The true celebration of Christmas, then, is the understanding that because Jesus is Immanuel, God with us, He is the answer to our deepest loneliness. Whatever we may be feeling, the truth is that we are never alone. That is God's promise. The last earthly words of Immanuel were, "and surely, *I am with you always*, to the very end of the age" (Matthew 28:20, emphasis added).

Crashing the Party

*B*efore God came to earth, He knew exactly what our ultimate response would be; yet He came anyway. In effect, He crashed His own party. Though we were content to live in the wonderful world He had given us, all the while neglecting and even defying Him, He would not allow this situation to continue. Knowing He would not be welcome, He came anyway.

Why? Because salvation couldn't be accomplished from a distance. For us to truly understand His love toward us, He had to move nearer to us, despite our hostility.

When a wild animal is stuck in a river, or entangled in some way, any attempts to rescue it are not welcomed; the wild creature sees such attempts as a threat. The animal kicks, bites, and otherwise tries to hinder the very rescue that would save it. Alas, we aren't much different.

When God came to us in the person of Jesus Christ, we were able to see that His purpose was deliverance not condemnation, love not judgment. But He had to get close enough to us and become visible to us in a way that would not instantly invoke fear in us. (The Old Testament appearances of God were frequently terrifying—awe-inspiring, but terrifying.) Simply put, He had to become one of us.

Love is a contact sport—that's what God so beautifully demonstrated. And He had to make contact to make the point (Romans 5:6–8).

But this also means that having made full contact with us, having smelled us up close, having tasted our worst cruelty firsthand, being fully and completely exposed to our self-centeredness, He wouldn't back out of the deal. He knew that He would never back out of the deal, but we needed to know it. *God with us* was proof of His commitment to us.

"We are no longer alone; God is with us," wrote Dietrich Bonhoeffer. "We are no longer homeless; a bit of the eternal home itself has moved into us. Therefore we adults can rejoice deeply within our hearts under the Christmas tree, perhaps more than the children are able. We know that God's goodness will once again draw near."[2]

What, then, is the appropriate response to the message: "Immanuel, God with us"? Is this just a phrase we hear, admire, and then pack away with our other Christmas decorations until next year?

No! There is only one proper response to someone who has literally died to be near you. It is to commit to be *with Him*!

We've all probably experienced being *around* someone without considering ourselves *with* them. Some people are so familiar to us that while they are around we don't really notice them. We look *past* them instead of *at* them, talk *around* them instead of *to* them. We can do this to our own spouses at times, or to our children. Friends, family, parents, co-workers can all fall prey to this insensitivity. And at some time or other most of us been the recipients of such distraction or neglect. We've been with a friend or someone we admired when along came someone of much greater importance and value than ourselves. Eyes and attention shifted, and although we remained physically present, we were treated as virtually absent.

Ignoring friends, family, and acquaintances is bad enough. But when we treat God as ornamental, we ignore the one who sacrificed His own Son, who gave His own life, to be intimate with us.

Christmas is a time to do more than decorate our homes and our trees and our gifts. It is a time to decorate our lives with His continual presence as we welcome the Savior moment by moment. Christmas is the ultimate celebration of the fulfillment of Isaiah's promise: "The Lord himself will give you a sign: The virgin will be with child and will give birth to a son, and will call him Immanuel."

When we feel alone or abandoned, we can cling to this precious truth. In fact, in those moments when we are most alone, we can be most aware of God's presence in our life, because He provides a perfect contrast to our present human condition. One friend is with us always. Immanuel, God with us—with me, with you—now!

This truth should fill our hearts with a real and lasting joy. It is good news—good news for all people. This news makes a Christmas truly "merry."

Rejoice! We're no longer home alone!

Reflection and Celebration

One thing that keeps us from entering into the true spirit of the incarnation is our incredible busyness during the Christmas holidays. Because of our many activities we do not spend quiet time alone with our Savior.

This year, make a special appointment to simply be alone with God. Set aside an hour, make yourself a cup of coffee or tea, and clear your mind of everything but His presence.

Try establishing a special place in your home for you and your family to quietly reflect during this busy time of year: perhaps a comfortable chair near a table, with a candle, a favorite Christmas decoration, and your family Bible. Use your imagination to make this special place attractive. If you have children, ask them for some ideas as well.

Instead of bringing your usual laundry list of requests, bring only a grateful heart and genuine thanksgiving for all He has done. Thank Him that He, the creator of heaven and earth, wanted to be closer to you. Thank Him for His grace and mercy that prompted His entrance into not only our world, but into your heart.

Celebrate Immanuel—God with you. If you are struggling with loneliness, take this special time to invite Him again into your presence. Thank Him that you are never alone, even when you feel alone.

And this Christmas, every time you hear, see, or read the name *Immanuel*, remember that, like rainbows, Immanuel is a perpetual reminder that we are no longer home alone!

FOUR

❄

For All the People

While strolling through a shop in the mall one Christmas season I happened to spy the word *Joy* dangling from the ceiling, slowly twirling in the air. Despite its gay coloring and festive holiday surroundings, however, the word seemed sadly out of place. No one looked the least bit joyful. I couldn't help but think how often, in similar fashion, happiness seems to drift in and out of most people's Christmas season like a decorative tumbleweed or a word adrift in space.

We have read the angelic declaration of joy recorded by Luke: "Do not be afraid. I bring you good news of great joy that will be for all the people" (Luke 2:10). But if we who believe in Jesus seriously ponder this message, we will find ourselves facing a dilemma. For while we certainly experience joy at remembering the entrance of our Lord into our world, that *wasn't* what the angel promised. He didn't promise that there would be good news just for Christians. The good news was to be "for *all* the people." But how could the birth of Jesus spell good news for everyone? Any search for the real Christmas spirit requires that we find the truth behind this incredible, angelic promise.

If news is only good for one race or one group of people or one segment of society, then it really isn't *good* news for all. It's good news for the recipients, but for the rest of us it's just news. Not long ago my neighbor drove up in a beautiful new SUV. We were both standing there admiring the vehicle when he told me that a relative had given it to him for "a steal." Now that was good news for my neighbor, and I rejoiced at his good fortune, but it wasn't my good news.

Good news is only good news *for you* if you're included in the benefits. I could appreciate my friend's good news, but I couldn't participate in the benefits. Now if his relative had *another* great car at a steal of a price . . . well, that might be good news for me.

Have you ever asked yourself what good news could affect all people equally, regardless of race, sex, income level, or location? I'll admit that I've spent quite a bit of time thinking about this, and several times during the process I despaired; it was just too difficult to find anything that was good news for all people equally. Initially, I thought of a cure for cancer. Surely that would be good news for all people. But then I realized that not everyone has cancer. Some have AIDS, heart problems, diabetes, Alzheimer's, or other diseases. So while a cure for cancer would be good news for those affected by cancer or for their loved ones, the benefits don't affect everyone equally.

Then I thought about war. Surely an end to all wars would be good news for everyone. Yet I quickly realized that, at any given time, many people are not at war or are not directly affected by the wars that are going on in different parts of the world. An end to all wars would be good news, but it wouldn't have an immediate effect upon everyone equally.

This was going to be more difficult than I had imagined.

Finally I was sure I had the answer: the elimination of poverty. Wouldn't that be universal good news? But of course there are millions of people who are not poor or are not directly affected by poverty. In fact, there are hundreds of millions, if not billions of people who are quite well off compared to everyone else. No, this good news simply wouldn't affect everyone equally.

It began to dawn on me that perhaps I had taken this familiar phrase, "good news of great joy that will be for all the people," for granted. For this news to be truly good news there could be no situation, no place, no people, no time, and no culture where it was *not* good news. So how could this "joy" we are supposed to experience truly be for "all the people?" What did the angel really mean? Was God engaging in divine hyperbole? Was He just being dramatic? Did "all the people" simply refer to all shepherds? Before I completely despaired, however, God reminded me of something I hadn't considered.

The Offer Is Open to Anyone

Think about all the offers you have heard and received in your life. How many of them were open to absolutely everyone who was alive and who would ever be alive in the future? Let's face it: all the offers we receive have built-in restrictions, limitations, and expiration dates attached to them.

A great example is the American ideal of freedom. Our country has for years stood as a beacon of hope to the peoples of the world. We offer freedom to all who are oppressed and seeking asylum. "Give me your tired, your poor, your huddled masses yearning to breathe free," is engraved on our Statue of Liberty. But there is one stipulation: they have to come to America to get that freedom. We can't export our freedom and make it available anywhere in the world. The offer, therefore, is not open to everyone, because not everyone can get to America. Do you begin to see the difficulty of finding any offer that affects all equally?

Amazing offers usually sound great until you read the fine print, where all the stipulations and qualifications are spelled out. Excitement quickly turns to disappointment when you learn that you have to buy something, or be a certain age, or fit a certain income level, or live in a certain place to be eligible. All of the many sweepstakes offered through the mail have fine print, which details who is really eligible and who is not and what the expiration date is. Chain stores also make great offers (buy-one-get-one-free), but they are always for a limited time and often have other stipulations (offer good only for the month of December, cannot be combined with any other offer). Even countries embroiled in civil war with rebel factions will sometimes declare a period of amnesty when rebels can be pardoned and reenter society without fear of retribution. Yet there is always a beginning and ending to this offer.

With all the cultures, languages, and geographical distances that separate us from one another, it is virtually impossible to make any offer universally and to have it always available. Humanly, it simply can't be done, no matter how hard we try. And some will always be better able to take advantage of any offer than others will. It's not fair, but it's life. And as we learn with maturity, life isn't always fair.

That's what makes this divine offer so unusual. This good news that will bring great joy transcends political boundaries, languages, customs, geography, status, income, race, religion, sex, and any other barrier. It is an offer that applies equally to each and every human heart and mind. There is no favoritism involved here, not even to the Jews. This wasn't "good news of great joy that shall be to all Jews," but *to all people.* And there is no expiration date—the offer is still good.

Our mission has always been to take this good news to every nation, which is why every people, country, language, and culture has been a target for Christian missionaries. It is just as important to share this good news with a person living in a primitive tribe in the jungles of South America as it is with those living in modern industrialized societies.

Jesus' birth didn't just offer good news to a certain group of people in a certain time and place. His birth and its implications ushered in good news for all the people who have ever been born or who ever will be born. That's why this "good news" means far more than we ever thought it did. It gives us a much deeper understanding of God's goodness.

God's Goodness and Grace

*D*uring my high school graduation ceremony, as each student's name was read, there was great cheering and whooping and hollering for the popular kids. When my name was read a lone cricket chirped mournfully. It was another painful reminder that my presence, or even my absence, was of little consequence.

I desperately yearned to know that somewhere, to someone, I was considered invaluable. When I was barely a teenager, I learned that the Christ child was born into our world in order that He might grow up to suffer and die for an insignificant guy like me. And while I knew He had come to die for everyone, I also understood that He would have gone through it all just for me. No one might have thought I was very important in high school, but all heaven rejoiced when I was granted entrance into His eternal kingdom.

I never had to be convinced that I was a sinner. My earliest visions of God, created by the churches I attended, provided a sobering picture. I always believed in an all-knowing, all-powerful, all-seeing God, but that knowledge never gave me much joy. In fact, I had a lingering feeling that if God paid too close attention to what I was doing He would make my life a living hell.

But God didn't send Gabriel, the Christmas angel, with bad news of a great judgment. He didn't come to tell us that God's had it with us and He's going to make an end to us — or worse. No, just the opposite. Jesus was born a Savior, not a Destroyer. He came to bring us great joy, not great destruction. Even after my sins sent Him to the cross, He only loved me back.

High school is now but a memory, as is college, but I still look forward into eternity and smile, knowing that I can never be insignificant if the God of heaven wants me to live with Him forever. The same is true for you. God didn't keep His love a secret from us. That's good news for *all* people.

When I first became a Christian, however, I thought that God's grace came with a ration card. Everyone got some, but you had to be careful that you didn't overdo it. So I approached God timidly at times, afraid my account might be overdrawn.

Yet instead of taking great delight in judging me for my shortcomings, of which there are many, God sent His Son to earth to settle accounts with Him on my behalf. He accepted Jesus' perfect life as a fitting payment for all my sins and my grace credit line was eternally extended.

I've spent a lot of time trying to convince people that there is a perfect, righteous God who loves them and forgives them. It's not an easy sell, strangely, but it is always good news.

This baby Savior would grow up in the midst of our sinful world. He would spend time with prostitutes and embezzlers, telling them the same thing He told the religious folks — "there's a place for you in My house, and I want you to come and live with Me. I know everything about you, and yet, I still want to be your Savior!" Good news for *all* the people!

❄

I am a dreamer; I have been all my life. Probably always will be. I am constantly dreaming of a better world, because the one I live in is so painful and unpleasant at times. I have a wonderful family and many wonderful friends and a life for which I am thankful. But this wonderful life cannot protect me from the death of loved ones, from sickness, from trials and tribulations. And I don't think I'm alone in my dreaming. I believe most people dream of a better life—a life without the pain and suffering.

To all who have dreamed of a better world, who have wondered what it would be like to live in a perfect world, with perfect relationships, in perfect peace, I say: there is good news! When God visited us from heaven, He offered empirical evidence that there is another world beyond this one. Our world would never, could never have produced our Savior; He had to come from a better place. This Savior who was born for you came to tell you what that other world is like and how you can become a citizen there someday.

Good News for Everyone!

*B*ut now we have come full circle. And I have to ask: Was the birth of Christ good news for Herod, who was jealous of Him and sought to kill Him? Was it good news for the Pharisees and scribes, who opposed and rejected Him? Yes it was, because although they may never have acknowledged it, they desperately needed a Savior.

Jesus is the only Savior anyone will ever have. He is Mother Theresa's savior, and he is Madonna's. The good news of great joy was for Madelyn Murray O'Hair as well as for Billy Graham. It was as much good news for Pilate and Herod as it was for Mary and Martha. Jesus was the Savior of the soldiers who crucified Him as well as Peter and Paul who worshiped Him.

The good news for the Hindus and the Buddhists and the Muslims is that Jesus is their Savior. In Acts 4:12 Peter says, "Salvation is found in no one else, for there is no other name under heaven given to men by which we must be saved." Jesus offers everyone salvation.

Although many people will never accept Him as their Savior, will never avail themselves of this good news, this in no way diminishes the character of the news. An act of kindness, even when it is snubbed, remains an act of kindness. Hope, even when it is rejected, is still hope.

Not long ago my brother-in-law was diagnosed with cancer. That was bad news. Fortunately, the doctors found the cancer in time, and he fully recovered—good news. Many forms of cancer are treatable, but only when they have been diagnosed, only when we know there is a problem. It is the same with God's good news. The good news highlights the bad news. The bad news is: we need a Savior. The good news is: we have one.

Madelyn Murray O'Hair, arguably the most famous, visible, and vocal atheist of the past few decades, vanished several years ago. When it was later discovered that she was dead, the victim of a murderer, her diaries were auctioned off to satisfy Internal Revenue Service claims against her estate. At least a half dozen times in her diaries four words appeared over and over. "Somebody, somewhere, love me."[1]

Somebody, somewhere did love her; He loved her so much that He died just for her. He wanted her to come and live with Him in His eternal kingdom forever. It was good news of a great joy that shall be for all the people, even Madelyn Murray O'Hair.

This good news is good no matter who you are, and the offer is the same no matter who you are. Whether you are Bill Gates or a street orphan in Brazil, whether you are the queen of England or a prostitute in New York, whether you have led a "charmed life" or are a three-strike prisoner who will never taste human freedom again, whether you have lived a wonderful life, trying to please God, or a life in defiance of God, the good news remains good.

Suddenly, in our search for the real spirit of Christmas, the joy of Christmas makes sense—a different joy, a greater joy, a permanent joy, the real joy! And even though our neighbors may not celebrate this joy with us, it is still good news for them.

> *But the angel said to them, "Do not be afraid. I bring you good news of great joy that will be **for all the people**. Today in the town of David a Savior has been born to you; he is Christ the Lord" (Luke 2:10–11, emphasis added).*

Reflection and Celebration

In our culture we are taught to respect everyone's race, religion, and culture. Such respect is good and proper. But to many, among them many Christians, this has come to mean keeping one's faith safely to oneself, to avoid offending anyone with the implications.

This Christmas, think of several of your non-Christian friends or friends of other faiths. Write down their names. After you've done that, ask yourself how the good news of Jesus' birth is good news to them. How might true joy enter their lives if they accepted this good news themselves? Ask God to show you a way to communicate this good news to them, not only through spoken words but also through acts of love and kindness. Make it your goal this year to find a creative new way to share the good news of great joy with those Jesus loves.

Each year Prison Fellowship sponsors the Angel Tree Project, which is a wonderful way to show the love and good news of Christmas to the children and families of prisoners. Along with your gifts, a card expressing the reason for your personal Christmas joy would be appropriate.

Helping to provide a traditional Christmas (a tree, presents, decorations) to a family or an individual in your community or neighborhood who has very little would also provide an opportunity to express to them the reasons behind your great joy and love in a card or short note. This might be even more effective if done anonymously.

I knew a couple who, every Christmas, would invite all their neighbors to a Christmas party with cookies, music, and all the cultural embellishments of the season that others have come to expect. But sometime during the party the husband would gather everyone around and read the Christmas story in Luke 2. No comments, no lecture, no sermons—just the simple story. A statement as simple as "This is what Christmas is really all about for me/us" at the end would creatively share the good news of a great joy!

The possibilities are endless!

FIVE

❄

Falling into Favor

*I*t began as just an ordinary day. The sun rose, the sleepy village stirred, and young Mary woke as she had every morning. Outside, the sounds of livestock filled the air, and human voices soon joined the din. Just an ordinary day and an ordinary girl, except that on this day all heaven was focused on her.

As she busied herself with her daily tasks, Mary had no way of knowing what was happening in the heavenly realms, where the angel Gabriel was being given his marching orders from God. Mary's ambitions were probably simple and similar to the other girls in her village. She would marry her betrothed, bear children, and raise a family. She had no way of knowing that on this day she would receive an unexpected visitor from an unexpected place with a completely unexpected announcement.

In Luke 1:28 we are told that the angel Gabriel suddenly "went to her." Did he come walking through the open door of her house? Through the wall? Did he stand at the entrance and announce himself? Did he look like a man, or was he brilliant and white? What did he sound like? How was he dressed? We don't know. The details are scarce. On this incredible day, it was a young Hebrew girl from Nazareth who was the focus of all heaven, not the messenger.

That Mary recognized he was an angel is clear, even though there is no mention of how she knew this. Perhaps the very sight of him made it crystal clear. If so, that same sight must have threatened to buckle her knees. Yet the angel's first words were not only comforting but highly flattering.

"Greetings, you who are highly favored! The Lord is with you" (Luke 1:28).

As positive as this message was, "Mary was greatly troubled at his words and wondered what kind of greeting this might be" (Luke1:29). Can we blame her? We view Mary in hindsight, with all the information given to us in the New Testament. But at the time this flattering message was delivered to her *by a heavenly being,* she was simply a young virgin from a small town engaged to a local carpenter. None of this made any sense to her. Who was she to be singled out in this miraculous way?

Gabriel allowed this greeting and its implications to sink into the young girl's heart and mind. He understood that his presence and message would be shocking, and he did not give her more information than she could bear.

Was she afraid? Probably. Because Gabriel's next words to her were "Do not be afraid."

Did she sink to her knees in confusion? After all, she had not yet been told that she would be the mother of the Messiah, the Son of God. She had only been told that she was highly favored and that the Lord was with her. But she *was* troubled at the words. Almighty God had sent an angelic messenger to her. What could this mean?

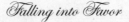

Mary knew that God loved her; He loved all Israel. That was clear from the scriptures she had heard and been taught as a child. Her faith in God was obviously strong. But why would God send an angel to her? And how would she be favored more than any other godly woman and, more importantly, why?

The angel's favorable greeting didn't provoke excitement and anticipation in Mary. It scared her to death.

The Message

*A*nd then comes the announcement of the ages:

> *"Mary, you have found favor with God. You will be with child and give birth to a son, and you are to give him the name Jesus. He will be great and will be called the Son of the Most High. The Lord God will give him the throne of his father David, and he will reign over the house of Jacob forever; his kingdom will never end" (Luke 1:30–33).*

While Mary understood the words, the enormity of the message was mind-boggling. Every faithful Jew awaited the coming of the Messiah, but this angel was telling her that she was going to be His mother. The fact that the long-awaited Messiah was coming was excitement enough for one lifetime, but to suddenly be told that you would be His mother—what do you do with a message like that? In fact, we still struggle with this message and its implications today.

That she would be the one to bear the Messiah was unthinkable. If she had done some great heroic, philan-thropic, or selfless deed, perhaps she might have said, "Oh, I know why I'm being favored, it's because of . . . ." But Mary had no such résumé. Her life had been quiet and uneventful, and she was barely more than a girl. Historians and com-mentators believe Mary was perhaps fourteen years old and some think she might have been as young as twelve. She was a peasant girl, living in a tiny insignificant village situated pic-turesquely on one of the southernmost slopes of the Lebanon mountain range. She was likely illiterate. Even her knowl-edge of the scriptures was limited to what she had heard in the synagogue and committed to memory. Her faith in God was great, and mature for her years, but yet to be tested. Although it soon would be.

In our world, when someone is greatly honored, there is always a reason. It is because they have accomplished some-thing magnificent or helped in some great endeavor. No one ever gives a high honor and while presenting it says, "This is for you, even though you have never done anything special. We're giving it to you *just because!*"

What had Mary accomplished in her young years to merit a greater blessing than any woman who had ever lived? Sarah, Esther, Naomi, Ruth, Hannah—the Old Testament is full of godly women who exercised strong faith and accomplished remarkable things for the Lord. Yet Mary's history is silent. If she hadn't done anything out of the ordinary, then why would God choose her for such an amazing blessing? She must have asked herself this question. Remember, she was "greatly trou-

bled" at the message. Mary certainly didn't feel she had done anything worthy of special attention to deserve this honor.

The truth is that Mary fell into favor. God chose her because it pleased Him to favor her. The reason for His favor rested in His grace, not in her amazing life. This doesn't mean Mary wasn't a wonderful and godly young woman; surely she was, as evidenced by her eventual response. It simply shows that God's grace and favor is undeserved, even by the best of us. Mary fell into favor. All of us do. Mary's "Magnificat," found in Luke 1:46–55, reiterates her humble state in contrast to the great honor being bestowed upon her. (Mary's hymn of praise is often called "The Magnificat" because in the Latin Vulgate translation the opening word of this passage is *Magnificat,* meaning "glorifies.")

Mary's calling was God's gift to her—His gracious favor. She received the gift of a baby who would grow up to be not only her son, but also her Savior. In what can only be described as a divine mystery, she would hold her Creator in her arms. His life would be in her hands. She would comfort, protect, feed, and love the One who had existed for all eternity. Yet she had done nothing that would entitle her to deserve this singular and spectacular honor—just as we have done nothing to deserve God's mercy.

The Messenger

If the message wasn't intimidating enough, consider the messenger—an angel. My teenage children would be terrified just getting called into the principal's office. We can only imagine what Mary felt when Gabriel appeared to her. Just to meet an angel would be intimidating, but Gabriel was one of God's most powerful and important angels. Only six months earlier, Gabriel had appeared to Zechariah, father of John the Baptist, and Zechariah had been struck speechless. Five hundred years earlier, the great and brave prophet Daniel had fallen to the ground in terror at the appearance of this same angel (Daniel 8:16–17).

We don't know what Gabriel looked like, or if he might have tempered his appearance to minimize the fear of this young girl. But this was certainly not a conventional meeting. Here was a messenger from God, a proof of the existence of the angelic and supernatural world, with a message from God for Mary's ears only.

In the Old Testament, angelic visitations weren't always a cause for celebration, so we can certainly understand why Mary might be troubled. But she was more than troubled. She was afraid—and Gabriel knew it.

> *"But the angel said to her, 'Do not be afraid, Mary, you have found favor with God. You will be with child and give birth to a son, and you are to give him the name Jesus. He will be great and will be called the Son of the Most High. The Lord God will give him the throne of his father David, and he will reign over the house of Jacob forever; his kingdom will never end'" (Luke 1:30–33).*

Mary was afraid, not only of this strange thing that would happen to her, but of all the implications.

What Would This Mean *for* Her?

*M*ary must have been a careful and reflective young woman, for she quickly moved beyond the glorious message and messenger to wonder what kind of greeting this might be. Mary was told she would have a baby boy and was commanded to name Him Jesus. Jesus, meaning "savior," was a rather common name among her people. But *this* Jesus would also be called "the Son of the Most High." Here is where the clouds began to lift and she probably needed to sit down.

She was going to give birth to God's Son!

Her son would inherit the throne of David and would reign over the house of Jacob forever—in other words, He would rule over a never-ending kingdom. She would be the mother of the long-awaited Messiah. Mother of God, mother of Messiah. The Messiah would be born in her. She would nurse her God. In all of human history, never would there be a greater honor for any woman, or a greater responsibility.

Could Mary really understand all of this at that moment? It is doubtful.

What Will This Require *from* Her?

*G*od slowly and carefully revealed to young Mary what He had purposed for her life. What was immediately clear, of course, was that her life would never be the same again. Everything would be drastically different because of this event, but she had no idea how different.

She would endure the temporary disdain of her betrothed Joseph when he discovered her pregnancy—before the angel appeared to him and told him what had occurred. She would suffer the shame of an unexplainable and unconcealable pregnancy in her hometown of Nazareth. She would bear her son in an animal pen, and her life and the life of her baby would be in danger as soon as He was born. She would be forced to flee to Egypt to escape Herod's assassination attempt on her son. And one day she would stand at the foot of a cross and watch her son being crucified.

In light of all this, some of us might wonder how the angel could claim that Mary was "favored." From our limited human perspective we might be tempted to cry out, "If that's what comes from being favored, please—favor someone else!"

Yet, for all the pain and suffering she would endure, God knew that Mary's blessing would be so deep, so rich, so powerful, that someday she would look back on her life and agree that she had indeed been "favored."

How much suffering, shame, or loss would we be willing to endure to be in the physical presence of our Lord for even a few minutes? Yet Mary nursed Jesus, comforted Him, protected Him, and was the recipient of the most perfect love any child ever gave to a parent.

Many parents are forced to endure a great deal of suffering with their own children, and often the children's response is not one of love and gratitude, but rebellion and hostility. While Mary would suffer things no other woman ever would, she would also experience such blessed holiness and fulfillment from her son and Savior that all would pale to insignificant.

Those who place their faith in Jesus, who follow Him and love Him, will suffer loss, ostracism, and hostility. Yet what we gain from Him so far exceeds what we lose or suffer that in the end we count it an inestimable privilege to have been brought into God's family. To quote Jim Elliot's famous words, "He is no fool who gives up what he cannot keep to gain what he cannot lose."

For now, of course, Mary had no idea what lay ahead or what would be required of her.

The Miracle

*W*ithout expressing any doubt about the truthfulness of what she had been told, Mary was understandably confused by the message.

> *"How will this be," Mary asked the angel, "since I am a virgin?" The angel answered, "The Holy Spirit will come upon you, and the power of the Most High will overshadow you. So the holy one to be born will be called the Son of God. Even Elizabeth your relative is going to have a child in her old age, and she who was said to be barren is in her sixth month. For nothing is impossible with God"* (Luke 1:34–37).

"How will this be?" she asked. Bless her heart, this young teenage girl was forced to talk about sex with an angel. Mary knew the facts of life, and the facts of life contradicted what the angel was saying. Didn't Gabriel understand the birds and the bees? He might just as well have told Mary that

Joseph was going to have a baby for all the sense that it made! It certainly wouldn't have been any more of a miracle!

Jewish betrothals were as binding as marriages, but couples did not come together as man and wife until the betrothal period was over. Mary and Joseph were still in that betrothal period, yet Gabriel seemed to indicate that soon she was to become pregnant. Mary knew she was still a virgin. Her question was a simple one: how?

Gabriel did not rebuke her, but gently explained that, in another miracle, the Most High would "overshadow" her. God would be the cause of her pregnancy, not through the ordinary means of sexual reproduction but through divine intervention. Furthermore, Gabriel revealed, she wasn't the only one who was going to have a miraculous birth. Mary's relative Elizabeth, who was well beyond childbearing age, was already six months pregnant.

How that news must have encouraged young Mary. Now she had someone to share her incredible experience with, someone who would understand. Elizabeth, an older woman to comfort, encourage, and provide an example to her, was a wonderful gift for Mary.

❄

With startling suddenness and surprise, Mary's quiet life was drastically changed forever. And yet God's call to us is always a surprise. We may be surprised that He wants us, or surprised that we want Him, or both. We may be surprised because we weren't seeking Him, or surprised that He was seeking us. Surprised that God wants to enter our life

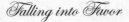

and do the impossible. Surprised that He wants to favor us with His mercy and grace.

The only thing that ever changes is the time and place and person. The process is always the same. God finds ways, often unexpected and sometimes unbelievable, to introduce us to the Savior, just as He did with Mary. The question is: How will we respond? How did Mary respond?

Mary's Ultimate Response: Acceptance and Submission

*M*ary's response is recorded in Luke 1:38.

> *"I am the Lord's servant," Mary answered. "May it be to me as you have said." Then the angel left her.*

No fighting against God's message, no more requests for clarifications, and no more questions. Whatever needed to be done, God would do. Mary's acceptance of and submission to God's plan for her was total and absolute. Her relative Elizabeth later put it eloquently when she described Mary's response to her angelic visitation:

> *"Blessed is she who has believed that what the Lord has said to her will be accomplished!" (Luke 1:45).*

Mary believed God. She didn't have all the answers, but she believed God. She didn't know how it would all work out, but she believed God.

Her example leaves us with the answer to one very big question: What does God want from *us*? Simply to return His favor. When a gift of amazing grace and love is given to us, the only proper response is to give faith and love back. It's true that God's love is perfect and holy, while ours can be impure, unreliable, shallow, and even disloyal at times. Yet this is what God seeks in return for the gift He gave us. Our acceptance and submission to Him are our gifts of love in gratitude for what He has given us in Christ, as surely as Mary's faith, acceptance, and submission were hers.

Mary fell into God's favor, and when she did, she did the right thing. She returned the favor. She blessed the One who blessed her. She received the gift and gave one back — her faith and acceptance.

What if Mary, the favored one, had said, "Wow! Hey, I'm really flattered, but I think I'll pass on this. Let someone else get this gift. I'm not sure I'm ready to be the mother of the Son of God"? The favor God wanted to bestow on her would have been forfeited if she had not been willing to step out in faith and receive the gift God had for her. And the same is true for us.

We have fallen into favor. And the Christmas spirit will fill our hearts when we realize that each of us receives the gift of Christmas the same way Mary did. Our faith is not an accomplishment; it is a "gift of God" (Ephesians 2:8–9). The grace we have received is not payment for good behavior, but an act of mercy.

As Jesus was born physically in Mary, so we have been born spiritually into Him. Gabriel's announcement echoes in us as well. We have been highly favored. The Lord is with us!

Reflection and Celebration

Put on some Christmas music and take a pleasant stroll down your own Christmas memory lane. In a journal, on your computer, or simply on a piece of paper list your three favorite Christmas presents of all time. Perhaps some old photo albums or home movies will help spur your memory.

Why was each of those gifts so special to you? Was it the gift itself or the person who gave it to you that made it special? And most importantly, why did someone give you those gifts? What do you think motivated them? Write down your answers to each of these questions.

Now, while the subject of gifts is fresh in your mind, turn your attention to the gift God gave you—the gift of Himself. Picture in your mind the Father delivering His precious Son into your hands. Ask yourself why He would give you such a precious gift. What surprises you most about His gift to you?

❄

SIX

The God We Thought We Knew

I must confess that I have a soft spot for many of our familiar holiday movies, but there is one of which I am especially fond. It is the old favorite TV special, *A Charlie Brown Christmas*. Charles Schulz's classic story of a little boy trying to find out what Christmas is all about in the midst of all the cultural embellishments of the season always touches me.

In this ageless story, Charlie Brown is feeling the emotions that so many of us experience as we approach the Christmas season. He knows he should be happier, and yet what seems to be bringing everyone else holiday happiness eludes him. The cultural expressions of the season seem plastic to him and leave him feeling empty. Lucy's unbridled greed in seeking real estate for a Christmas present and the blinking electric Christmas lights on Snoopy's doghouse conspire to deplete his "holiday" feelings. Even his attempt to get into the Christmas spirit by directing the Christmas play fails.

At his lowest point, when Charlie despairs of ever finding out what Christmas is all about, his friend Linus quietly reminds him that Christmas is really all about the birth of the Savior, Jesus. This epiphany changes Charlie Brown's entire attitude as he joyfully discovers that Christmas is far more than he ever thought it was. His views of Christmas, he learns, have been all wrong.

One of the most amazing truths of Christmas is that God's entrance into our world shows us that much of what we think we know about God is wrong. (Mankind has misunderstood God from the very beginning, so it is of little surprise that we still do.) In fact, this is one of the reasons that many modern-day Charlie Browns still fail to enter into the true Christmas spirit. Thinking they know the "real story" of Christmas, they tend to ignore it rather than examine it, leaving the Christmas story too soon. They have failed to appreciate what God was showing us when He came into our world. But closer inspection reveals an event that makes no earthly or human sense.

How Well Do We Know God?

How would we have foreseen the incarnation? What would we have anticipated?

Because we see God as the Almighty Jehovah who is too glorious to look upon, wouldn't we have expected Him to enter our world with ostentatious fanfare and world-stopping commotion?

Well, didn't He, you might reply. After all, angels announced the news to the shepherds. That's certainly fanfare! Yes, but they didn't announce the news to everyone—not even to all shepherds

What about the Magi, you might ask. True, a small group of Magi arrived from the east, following the star they had seen in the sky, but they were a mere token compared to the millions of people who inhabited the earth at the time.

Well, then, what about the star? Did everyone notice that one particular star? Did they understand the significance of that celestial sign? Of all the stars in the sky, did they focus on that one star above all others? It is doubtful. How many people even noticed the sky?

God did not choose to enter our world in the all-powerful city of Rome, but in the tiny town of Bethlehem. He was not born in a palace, but in a stable for animals. His royal entourage was not regally dressed nobles and princes, but common beasts of burden. His human parents were not royalty, but peasantry, His royal raiment nothing but common cloth.

Yes, I believe we would expect the God of the universe to reveal Himself on earth with an all-out, budget-breaking PR blitz. Instead, God voluntarily gave up the glory He deserved, both on earth and in heaven, and chose to live most of his life in obscurity.

We would assume that a God who is all-powerful would exercise that power to protect His reputation and personal glory. And God would certainly not allow His puny creation to treat Him with defiance. With His perfect righteousness and holiness God would come in judgment to a creation that had mocked His law and ignored His commandments. But He didn't.

We are tempted to say that God didn't act "naturally." It doesn't seem natural to us that a perfect deity would treat His creation with so much love and grace after they had treated Him so badly. We can't even imagine a God who would love enough to allow Himself to be treated with contempt and disdain. But that's just the point. He did act naturally. Not once in the magnificent incarnation did God act outside of His divine character. We just didn't know Him as well as we thought we did. In fact, when God put Himself at our disposal, we didn't even recognize Him.

We knew many things about God, but our understanding was black and white. And when He came, He overwhelmed us with the brilliant colors of His divine character.

We thought we knew God, but the incarnation proved us wrong.

If God Visited the Planet

One of the most popular and cherished human ideas is that we can seek and find God. But if you had known ahead of time that God was planning to visit our planet, where would you have expected to find Him? Where would you have started looking for Him? Would you have thought of looking for a baby? Would your first stop have been an animal stall? Would you have gone to the home of a carpenter to find the designer of the universe? Wouldn't you have been looking for an angelic type of being, powerful, awesome, terrifying, and unapproachable?

If you knew that God planned to announce His coming to His world, would you ever have put a rude and crude bunch

of shepherds anywhere near the top of the "to be notified" list?
If you knew that God was going to visit your planet, what do
you think He would plan for His first year on earth, or His first
five years? What kind of splash would He make to get the
world's attention? Who would He speak to? How would He go
about instituting change in this world He had created so perfectly, and which we had so dreadfully messed up? How would
He use His awesome infinite power? How would He display
His omnipotence, His omniscience, and His holiness?

Knowing what we think we know about God, we probably could come up with thousands of ideas, many of them rea-
sonable and logical and even creative. But would we think to
have Him humble Himself before His creation by being born
a tiny vulnerable baby and spending His first days on this
earth in an animal stall, unable to speak or even communicate
any but His most basic human needs?

Christmas celebrates the awesome and amazing fact that
God is grander, wiser, and more mysterious than we could
have ever imagined.

We Can't Find God by Ourselves

*I*f there is one thing we learn at Christmas, it is that
our understanding of God was so woefully inadequate that we could never have hoped to find Him on our
own. How can you find a God you can't even truly understand? Which leads to the next logical question: How would
a God of perfect glory and awesome splendor reveal Himself?

In his best-selling book, *The Jesus I Never Knew*, Philip Yancey contrasts the humility of Jesus' entrance onto our planet with the prestigious entrance of the British royal family.

> In London, looking toward the auditorium's royal box where the queen and her family sat, I caught glimpses of the . . . ways rulers stride through the world: with bodyguards, and a trumpet fanfare and a flourish of bright clothes and flashing jewelry. Queen Elizabeth II had recently visited the United States, and reporters delighted in spelling out the logistics involved: her four thousand pounds of luggage included two outfits for every occasion, a mourning outfit in case someone died, forty pints of plasma, and white kid-leather toilet seat covers. She brought along her own hairdresser, two valets, and a host of other attendants. A brief visit of royalty to a foreign country can easily cost twenty million dollars.
>
> In meek contrast, God's visit to earth took place in an animal shelter with no attendants present and nowhere to lay the newborn king but a feed trough. Indeed, the event that divided history, and even our calendars, into two parts may have had more animal than human witnesses. A mule could have stepped on him."[1]

The British royalty are merely human beings, and look at the pomp and circumstance with which they arrive on the scene. In light of that, when we think that God was planning a visit to His own creation, with all of eternity to plan the event, we can't look at the Christmas story and make sense out of it. Everything about Christmas is totally unexpected. In retrospect, of course, we see His infinite wisdom; but even then, we see this only with His divine help and the eyes of faith. God is so much different than we imagined Him to be. We are not surprised that He is greater in glory than we could ever imagine. But the discovery that He is greater in humility is too great a leap for us to take. God and humility seem such opposite terms. Only in His infinite wisdom and mercy—and in the incarnation—could they ever be reconciled.

One of the common tools of criminal investigators is to create a profile. By studying the habits and patterns and behaviors of a given criminal, they can get a good idea of what he is thinking, why he acts the way he does, and sometimes even where he lives. By this process, they narrow down their search for who this criminal might be. In doing this, they apply human wisdom and logic to the sticky problem of human nature. They understand people because they are people themselves—they share the same human nature. Because they do, they can deduce how someone will act, and at times predict their actions.

But all these human nature tools are useless when we come to God. Christmas reveals to us that the idea of God we had developed was woefully inadequate.

Confused by Humility

When we read of God's divine power and authority so clearly demonstrated in the Old Testament, we quite logically expect God to react and behave in that manner. When we remember His displays of His presence and power in burning bushes, fire by night, cloud by day, thunder, lightning, and many other awesome manifestations, we are sure that when He comes to visit us He will use these same methods. Familiarity with what He has done in the past blinds us to what He intended on that first Christmas.

As J. B. Phillips writes, "Whenever familiarity breeds contempt there is potential danger. The particular danger which faces us as Christmas approaches is unlikely to be contempt for the sacred season, but nevertheless our familiarity with it may easily produce in us a kind of indifference. The true wonder and mystery may leave us unmoved; familiarity may easily blind us to the shining fact that lies at the heart of Christmastide."[2]

Had you lived in first-century Israel and known Mary and Joseph, or been one of the shepherds or Magi, you might have been able to cradle God in your arms. You could have easily overpowered His tiny arms and legs as He lay there vulnerable and helpless.

Helpless God.

Vulnerable God.

Hungry God.

Tired God.

None of these phrases would have any meaning to us had Christmas never occurred. Indeed, we would consider them blasphemous. We could simply not imagine these words used in connection with perfect Deity. But because of the incarnation they have meaning.

Even more difficult for us to comprehend would be the reason God made Himself helpless, vulnerable, hungry, and tired. We could in a finite sense understand God's power and His glory and His Majesty, but nothing could prepare us to understand the depth of His love as demonstrated in His unimaginable humility. His actions on that wonderful day we celebrate every year as Christmas displayed love better than any definition could ever hope to do.

"For God so loved the world that he gave his one and only Son, that whoever believes in him shall not perish but have eternal life. For God did not send his Son into the world to condemn the world, but to save the world through Him" (John 3:16–17). These familiar verses are the Magna Carta of the incarnation, the one and only possible explanation for the unthinkable.

❄

*C*hristmas is God unrecognized, God unexpected, God misunderstood. It is also, to our utter amazement and joy, God delightfully revealed. Though it had been prophesied, His birth was nothing we expected, and more than we could have hoped. His humility touches us deeply, revealing to us the depth of God's love. His entire life, from His humble birth to His humiliating and agonizing death on the cross, is proof of the love He has for us.

We could never have sought such a God, because we never understood Him and would never have recognized Him. So He had to come looking for us. That is the inescapable conclusion of the Christmas story.

God tracked us down, each and every one of us. He came to find us and reveal Himself to us because He wanted us to know Him. He wanted us to know the depth of His love for us. Words weren't enough. Only actions could communicate the extent to which He would go to bring us back home.

Do you want to get into the Christmas spirit? Cuddle a baby close to you. Let those tiny fingers grab yours. Snuggle the child against you and feel its complete dependence upon you. Experience the fragile vulnerability of that precious little life and you will begin, in a small sense, to understand the incarnation. Your God poured Himself into just such a frail life and made it His own. He allowed Himself to be dependent upon His creation, to be at their mercy. Then ask yourself: What kind of love would compel a perfect, all-powerful being to do such a thing?

We can never hope to capture the Christmas spirit and make it our own unless we understand that God is so much greater than we ever thought He was.

We thought we knew all about God. The incarnation proved us wrong.

Reflection and Celebration

At times, we enter into the Christmas spirit best by means of a sanctified imagination. We always view the wonder of the incarnation with the benefit of hindsight. And because we do, it is easy to take all the miraculous elements of Christmas for granted. This year, don't!

Imagine what the entrance of the Creator of the universe into our world would have been like if He had given you the assignment of planning the event. With what you know of God's glory, power, and unapproachable holiness, what plan would you have devised? What spectacular promotion would you have envisioned?

What false assumptions about God might have steered you in the wrong direction? How would your plan differ from His, and why? What part of God's eternal perfect nature would have confused you?

At the end of this exercise, ask yourself how God is greater than you imagined Him to be. How did He surprise you? What does this incredible Christmas story teach you about God that you could never have learned otherwise?

This Christmas try to discover some new insight into God's perfect nature in the Christmas story. Look for the unexpected, the humanly illogical, and discover anew the God you thought you knew.

SEVEN

❄

Givers or Receivers?

*I*t was exactly twelve days before Christmas and we had just finished stuffing the special Christmas stocking with the secret message and ornament. As I loaded our three young children into the van, they vainly struggled to suppress excited giggles. A few doors from the home we were targeting, I stopped, turned off the headlights, and gave the kids their final instructions in whispered conspiratorial tones.

"OK, Christi is the oldest, so she gets to put the stocking on the door tonight." Andrew moaned. "Tomorrow night it will be Andrew's turn." Andrew grinned. "And the next night Katie's. You can all go with Christi. But—and this is very important—you have to be quiet, and *very* sneaky."

Few children in this world can resist getting excited when they hear their parents tell them they can be sneaky. General Christi turned to her younger sister and whispered her own form of encouraging words. "Katie, don't talk!"

"I won't talk!" Katie replied.

"You ALWAYS talk!" Christi retorted.

"Yeah, Katie, so be quiet," warned Andrew.

Katie nodded solemnly, biding her time until the day when she could be the general.

Stealthily they jumped out into the darkness. (I can still see them crouching and sneaking along.) Christi hung the stocking, rang the doorbell, and they all raced back. They leaped into the van and we were off before the front door opened. On the way home, the kids laughed, replayed their exciting adventure, and anticipated the eleven nights yet to go. Each night the routine and the house was the same: sneak in, hang the gift stocking on the door, and dash away. Then on Christmas morning we would return with a dozen dough-nuts and sing "We Wish You a Merry Christmas," revealing ourselves as their Secret Santas.

Years earlier we had been the recipients of this activity called "The Twelve Days of Christmas" from a wonderful family in our church. On the first night of the twelve nights before Christmas the doorbell rang, and when we answered, we discovered no one was there—but there was a stocking hanging on the door. Along with a gift, the stocking con-tained a message telling us, in poetic form, that each night until Christmas we would receive another special gift from our "secret Christmas friend," each corresponding to the Twelve Days of Christmas.

We promptly adopted this simple act of kindness, which is as much fun for us as for those we target. And every year

since, we have done "The Twelve Days of Christmas" for a different family. It is a wonderful Christmas tradition and one of our children's fondest Christmas memories.

'Tis the Season To Feel Good

*T*he Twelve Days of Christmas" is only one of many Christmas giving activities we have been involved with over the years. We have helped provide a tree and presents for needy families in our community, bought gifts for the children of prisoners, paid for a well for a small village in Asia with proceeds from a garage sale, made up shoe boxes filled with Christmas goodies for children all over the world, and many other giving opportunities. And we loved every minute of it.

It made my wife, Annette, and me feel good. It made our children feel good. It made the people we were targeting with our Christmas project feel good.

I'm sure you've enjoyed similar satisfaction as you've been involved in some act of charity or kindness during the Christmas season. Surely this is the true spirit of Christmas. Or is it?

At Christmas it seems we are offered more opportunities to do good than at any other time of the year. Countless charities vie for ways to help us become true Christmas givers. These charities know that generous impulses don't always last much beyond Christmas Day, so they hit us early and often. For eleven months of the year we may be fairly apathetic to the sad plight of the needy, but at Christmas we go out of our way to be generous.

Our modern culture has drilled into us the message that the true spirit of Christmas is in giving to others. This message is not only commercially successful, but works on an emotional level as well. It is personified in Ebenezer Scrooge, who awakened to his miserly nature in the nick of time in Charles Dickens's famous story, *A Christmas Carol*.

Although I always get goose bumps when Ebenezer Scrooge sends the turkey and gifts to the Cratchett home on Christmas morning, the underlying theme is that the true spirit of Christmas is found in kindness and generosity. Scrooge is transformed when he ends his miserly ways and embraces the true spirit of Christmas by becoming generous, and thus a better person.

Has the real Christmas story, the entrance of God into our world, prompted this spirit of giving? In many cases, yes. But in some cases, no. Giving is certainly a wonderful way to respond to Christ's love at Christmas, but is it the true spirit of Christmas? It is interesting to note that Dickens's tale of crusty old Scrooge has probably done more to form our notions of what the Christmas spirit is than the account of Christ's birth in the Gospels.

Christmas is the chance for many to rescue their self-esteem—to prove the goodness of their character to themselves, as well as to others. Our gifts of time and money to help those less fortunate than ourselves convince us that we really are good people. After all, just look at our generosity.

I hasten to add that these acts of kindness *are* truly wonderful. I don't wish to undermine or minimize them in any way. But did you ever wonder why the sad plight of others receives such special attention from us during Christmas, and such scant attention the rest of the year? Why don't we help others and demonstrate kindness with the same intensity January through November?

A Christmas Carol Versus the Christmas Story

Is the real Christmas spirit about giving? Is that the message of the incarnation?

James reminds us, "Every good and perfect gift is from above, coming down from the Father of the heavenly lights, who does not change like shifting shadows" (James 1:17). And John 3:16 tells us that the incarnation was about God's giving. "For God so loved the world that he gave his one and only Son . . ." (John 3:16).

So Christmas *must* be about giving, right? Yes, but we are overlooking an important point: Who is doing the giving, and who is doing the receiving? The biblical account of Jesus' entrance into our world stresses that we are the unlikely recipients of a divine gift of which we are totally and completely unworthy. The giver in the story is God, not us. We are the receivers who did nothing to deserve this tremendous gift. It is a far more powerful story than that of Ebenezer Scrooge, but alas, not as flattering. Dickens's tale makes us feel better about ourselves and offers the hope that even the worst among us — even an Ebenezer Scrooge — can become a better person through unselfishness and generosity.

In an article entitled, *"The God We Hardly Knew,"* William Willimon suggests that Dickens's wonderful story is "more congenial to our favorite images of ourselves" than is the story of the incarnation. He goes on to say that we are better givers than getters not because we are generous but "because we are proud, arrogant people." He continues:

> The Christmas story — the one according to Luke, not Dickens — is not about how blessed it is to be givers but about how essential it is to see ourselves as receivers. . . . It tells us of an unimaginable gift from a stranger, a God whom we hardly even knew. This strange story tells us how to be receivers. The first word of the church, a people born out of so odd a nativity, is that we are receivers before we are givers. . . . It's tough to be on the receiving end of love, God's or anybody else's. It requires that we see our lives not as our possessions, but as gifts. "Nothing is more repugnant to capable, reasonable people than grace," wrote John Wesley a long time ago. . . . This is often the way God loves us: with gifts we thought we didn't need, which transform us into people we don't necessarily want to be.[1]

Christmas *is* an appropriate time to express the love of Christ through special giving and acts of compassion. It is not

the act we must scrutinize, but the motivation and the goal behind it. Is it our own self-esteem we are cultivating at this time of year, or are we expressing gratitude for the grace we have been shown?

Celebrating a Gift

*E*ach year when I celebrate with my precious wife, Annette, the anniversary of our marriage, I give her a special gift. Sometimes it is a quiet dinner at a nice restaurant; sometimes it is a special piece I have written for her; and sometimes it is a special vacation at one of our favorite places. I never fail to spend money or to sacrifice in some tangible way to express my deep joy in being married to her.

But I do not celebrate how good a catch I was, or how lucky Annette is to have married me. I do not recount all the wonderful things I have done for her over the years. There would be little joy in that for either of us. What I celebrate is a gift, pure and simple—one I received from the loving heart of my God and heavenly Father. I remind myself that of all the men this amazing woman could have been given to, He gave her to me. And of all the men my wife could have chosen to be her husband, she chose me. I am a humble and grateful receiver. There is no pride in my celebration, only lasting and sincere gratitude and joy. So on our anniversary I celebrate a gift, not a personal accomplishment.

This is the way we are to celebrate Christmas—as receivers. It is the Christmas contradiction. On the day

famous for giving to others, we are to celebrate being helpless but grateful receivers. It is gratitude born of a love so
deep that it must be expressed.

Celebrating Receiving

*W*hy was Bethlehem chosen to be the birthplace of
our Lord? Was it a large, successful, and significant
city? No, just the opposite. "But you, Bethlehem Ephrathah,
though you are small among the clans of Judah, out of you will
come for me one who will be ruler over Israel, whose origins
are from of old, from ancient times" (Micah 5:2, emphasis
added). Bethlehem was honored in spite of its insignificant
size and lack of importance.

Were the shepherds chosen to receive the angelic
announcement because they were men of honorable character and spiritual depth? No, we've already learned the kind of
reputation most shepherds had.

What of Mary and Joseph? Were they chosen to be the
human parents of Jesus because of their great achievements
and the opportunities they could offer Him? As we've seen,
Mary, though certainly a godly young woman, had not had
time to achieve great things in life, and Joseph was a simple,
though godly, carpenter. They did not earn the right to
become the parents of Christ by virtue of their character or
accomplishments; they too were receivers. Mary exalts not in
what she has done, but that "the Mighty One has done great
things *for me*" (Luke 1:49, emphasis added).

The obvious spirit of that first Christmas was one of being blessed, of having received mercy and grace from God.

It is tempting to focus on my kindness, thoughtfulness, and goodness as I scurry about trying hard to make everyone's Christmas special. Perhaps this is why the true spirit of Christmas remains elusive. Gratitude seeks to respond to the one who has given to you. But when you begin to focus on your own giving, you seek a reaction from the one you have given to. This does not always breed contentment, since not everyone will be as grateful as we might hope. Nor will our gifts always be completely appreciated.

Can we celebrate receiving God's indescribable gift and still do acts of kindness and charity at Christmas? Certainly! It would be strange if we didn't. But what motivates our acts of kindness will make all the difference. The act of kindness or generosity itself will look identical to onlookers regardless of our motivations. But we—and God—will know the difference.

In our attempt to find the true spirit of Christmas, then, we need to be able to identify its counterfeit. A variety of things can make us feel good during the holidays, but many of them are cultural messages. The true message of Christmas humbles us. It shows us for what we are: poor, blind, deaf, and dumb receivers.

So this season when you are preparing your gift giving and your charitable Christmas projects, focus not on what you are able to give, whether great or small, but on what you have received. Let the grace and mercy you have experienced at His hands first fill your heart, and then flow through you to others. In so doing, you are inviting others to join in your grateful celebration. Allow yourself to experience the wonder and joy of gratitude in this holy season. Feel what Mary, Joseph, the shepherds, the Magi, Simeon, and Anna must have felt.

We are both receivers and givers at Christmas. Let's just remember which comes first.

Reflection and Celebration

In Frank Capra's beloved holiday classic, *It's a Wonderful Life*, George Bailey is given the opportunity to experience what life would have been like if he had never been born. Revisiting his past, and his past family members and acquaintances, he is shocked to learn how he made a difference in so many people's lives. It is a shocking revelation to him, reminding him that even though his own life doesn't seem worth living anymore, his life has been very blessed.

If you've never seen this movie, buy it or rent it, and enjoy this wonderful touching classic. If you've seen it before, take it out, dust it off, and watch it one more time. Only this time, when the movie is over, take a few moments and try to imagine how many ways your life would be different if Jesus had never been born. It is a good exercise to remind us of how much we have received because a Savior was born to us.

Perhaps you and your family could do "The Twelve Days of Christmas" for another family. If you want more details on what this involves and how to do it, visit my Web site at: www.danschaeffer.com.

And the next Christmas compassion project you are involved with, *remember*: you can give because you first received. Your gift of time or treasure is merely an extension of His gift of love and grace to you. Christmas is first about receiving God's great love, and then about giving.

EIGHT

❄

Beware the
Christmas Grinches

One of the most popular holiday movies is Dr. Seuss's children's tale, *The Grinch Who Stole Christmas*. It is the gentle story of a miserable Grinch who tries to steal the joy of the Christmas season from the Whos down in Whoville. The Grinch personifies all those who view Christmas with disdain, and he joins a long list of those who, like Scrooge, have found Christmas a cause to grumble.

Consider Upton Sinclair, one of the more articulate grumblers of the past. "Or consider Christmas—could Satan in his most malignant mood have devised a worse combination of graft plus bunkum than the system whereby several hundred million people get a billion or so gifts for which they have no use, and some thousands of shop clerks die of exhaustion while selling them and every other child in the Western world is made ill from overeating—all in the name of the lowly Jesus?"[1]

Each Christmas season the Grinches appear and make themselves heard. As loudly as we celebrate and rejoice, they protest, object, and accuse. Everything about Christmas seems to infuriate them. But it isn't merely the cultural celebration of Christmas that offends them, the buying and selling, the endless variations of "White Christmas," the overdoing and overeating. No, the real target of their anger is the story behind it all. Why? Because the story is presented as truth, not myth. And they are sharp enough to know that this truth has serious consequences.

There is no danger in not believing in Santa. There is considerable and eternal danger in not believing in Jesus.

We often forget that while Christmas is a comfort for those of us who believe in Christ, it is a threat to many who do not. And each person who feels threatened by Christmas has a spiritual ancestor in the Christmas story.

The Original Grinch

*O*pposition to the miracle of Christmas began even before our Savior was born. In fact, if it weren't for God's divine providence, the Christ child would have been murdered before the Magi ever reached Him. The one who wanted to stop Christmas in its tracks is a familiar Christmas villain named Herod.

Herod is missing from the manger scene, but not by his choice. He would have been more than happy to find the little baby Jesus, but for his own purposes. "Go and make a careful search for the child," he told the Magi. "As soon as you find him, report to me, so that I too may go and worship him" (Matthew 2:8). His words ring with sincerity, but his heart was another matter. He wanted to stop the celebration before it ever began.

Herod was the first organized opposition to Jesus, and he provides the other Christmas story, the unhappy Christmas story of fear, jealousy, and ruthless persecution. Herod is the reminder that God sent His Son into a world that really didn't want Him, a world that was threatened by Him and would eventually finish what Herod started. Herod is every man and woman who ever rebelled against God and His rule over his or her life.

Some of us eventually join the angels, the shepherds, the Magi, and Simeon and Anna in rejoicing in His arrival. Others remain with Herod, at least in spirit. And while many may wish Christians no evil, they also wish Jesus no power in or over their lives. They desperately hope He is not who He said He was, for then he *would* threaten their lives.

"We have become so accustomed to the idea of divine love and of God's coming at Christmas that we no longer feel the shiver of fear that God's coming should arouse in us," wrote Dietrich Bonhoeffer. "We are indifferent to the message, taking only the pleasant and agreeable out of it and forgetting the serious aspect, that the God of the world draws near to the people of our little earth and lays claim to us. The coming of God is truly not only glad tidings, but first of all frightening news for everyone who has a conscience."[2]

Is fear an appropriate reaction to the message of Christmas? It can be. If someone has written God out of their life, deemed Him ultimately insignificant in the grand scheme of things, the message of Christmas can provoke a healthy fear. It raises the profound question: If God *did* come to earth, what are the consequences of my disbelief or disobedience?

Jesus came to bring an offer from His heavenly Father, an incredibly merciful and gracious offer. But it is also a costly offer. It costs our allegiance, our devotion, our obedience, and our worship. This is the sticking point! And this is why it is impossible to remain neutral toward Jesus. For if He truly was the Son of God come to our world to offer us salvation, then He cannot be ignored. He and His claims may be hated, denied, rejected, or repudiated, but He cannot be ignored.

Ravi Zacharias, in his book *Questions I Would Like To Ask God*, quotes popular talk show host Larry King who was once asked the question, "If you could select any one person across all of history to interview, who would it be?" Mr. King's answer was that he would like to interview Jesus Christ. When the questioner asked him, "And what would you like to ask him?" King replied, "I would like to ask him if he was indeed virgin-born. The answer to that question would define history for me." When Ravi Zacharias wrote to a mutual friend and requested permission to use that response, Larry King gave that permission and said, "And tell him I was not being facetious."[3]

Two thousand years after His birth, what to do with Jesus is still a struggle for many, and the celebration of His birth annually accentuates their struggle. His claims lay like a dark shadow over their lives. They can ignore Him for long periods of time, but each year Christmas brings the thorny subject up again. On some level and to varying degrees they know that they ignore Him at their own peril, but to accept Him will demand changes they just can't accept.

Herod was afraid of Jesus. He was afraid that this child's life would somehow threaten his own, and He was right. But He feared Jesus for the wrong reasons.

Herod knew nothing of the angels and the shepherds. And had the Magi come to Jerusalem asking only where the baby Jesus had been born, it is doubtful Herod would have been greatly concerned. But when they said, "Where is the one who has been born king of the Jews? We have come to worship him," Herod was filled with jealousy and fear. It wasn't the angels or the shepherds or the star or the Magi that troubled Herod. None of these, to his mind, posed a threat to him. It was only the mention of the title "king of the Jews" that stirred fear in the heart of the king. And that is not surprising.

Herod's cruelty was legendary. Over the years, he had eliminated by assassination every possible rival to his throne and his power, including his wives and his sons. Herod loved his power and clung to it tenaciously, so he was rightfully wary of any who might lay a claim to it. So when Herod saw in this new king a threat to his position, however small that might seem at the time, he dealt with this threat as he had dealt with all others.

"When Herod realized that he had been outwitted by the Magi, he was furious, and he gave orders to kill all the boys in Bethlehem and its vicinity who were two years old and under, in accordance with the time he had learned from the Magi" (Matthew 2:16).

But Jesus didn't just challenge Herod's position. He challenges all who believe they can live independent of the rule of God, all who are ultimately unwilling to bow before the Carpenter of Galilee, the Son of the Living God. Jesus will not leave us alone. He will pursue us, and we will either welcome the pursuit or be revulsed by it.

Modern-day Grinches are being pursued by the Babe in the manger, and because they aren't willing to receive Him, they must reject Him. Instead of being angry at their tirades, we must begin to understand what is at stake and why they are so adamantly opposed to Him.

The Great Defeat

*T*he life of Jesus drowns the accomplishments of Herod in a sea of insignificance. In fact, the only reason most people remember Herod at all is in relationship to Jesus. This king who built splendid palaces and thought himself a giant among men has been reduced to a footnote in history by the birth of a baby in a manger.

History fondly remembers Joseph, a carpenter, and Mary the mother of Jesus, but Herod's greatest contribution was to provide a black backdrop against which Jesus might shine the brighter. Herod wanted to defeat this rival king — but the story of Christmas is that he lost. His was the first loss in a string of losses that have continued for 2000 years.

For many, it is difficult to surrender to Jesus. Because surrender it is. We must surrender our will, our life, our pride and lay them at the feet of the Babe. We have to admit defeat. We cannot save ourselves, and we cannot compete with Him. We need Him. At first this seems so terribly unfair, because we have yet to understand that we are surrendering to perfect love and grace.

Several years ago *Time* magazine commissioned author and novelist Reynolds Price to write an article on Jesus for the new millennium. He entitled it "Jesus of Nazareth: Then and Now," and in it he noted:

"The memory of any stretch of years eventually resolves to a list of names, and one of the useful ways of recalling the past two millenniums is by listing the people who acquired great power. Muhammad, Catherine the Great, Marx, Gandhi, Hitler, Roosevelt, Stalin and Mao come quickly to mind. There's no question that each of those figures changed the lives of millions and evoked responses from worship through hatred. It would require much exotic calculation, however, to deny that the single most powerful figure—not merely in these two millennium but in all human history—has been Jesus of Nazareth."[4]

And when H. G. Wells, the famous British historian, was asked which person left the most permanent impression upon history, he replied that you needed to judge a person based upon historical standards. "By this test," Wells concluded, "Jesus stands first. I am a historian, I am not a believer. But I must confess as a historian that this penniless preacher from Nazareth is irrevocably the very center of history. Jesus Christ is easily the most dominant figure in all of history."[5]

It is difficult to worship the Savior and at the same time exalt yourself. One must either surrender to Him or compete with Him. Herod sought to compete, and he lost.

Yet Jesus came to show people just like Herod—and Herod himself—how important they are to Him. What greater importance can anyone have than that their God wants a relationship with them? So those who debunk Christmas because it threatens their own view of themselves, who refuse to be humbled before Christ, deserve our deepest pity.

One of the beautiful truths of Christmas is that we stand insignificant before our awesome Creator, who came to give us greater significance than we could ever hope to achieve on our own.

A Case of . . . Jesus Jealousy

*H*erod probably did not have a friend in the world, but he did have power over people. If someone rose up who might steal away any allegiance from him, his rule could be in danger. Then came the Magi wondering where the new king of the Jews had been born.

The Magi hadn't come to worship the aged and experienced political campaigner, Herod, but an infant king. They had brought no gifts to the esteemed and eminent King of Judea, but laid valuable gifts at the feet of the child. As a final insult, after completing their mission the Magi left Jerusalem without so much as a "by your leave" to Herod the Great, King of Judea, Galilee, Iturea, and Traconitis.

Herod was jealous of Jesus. And even today Jesus provokes this same reaction in many. How many spouses, friends, or parents become jealous of the attention Jesus gets from those who used to give them all their love and devotion? A husband, jealous of his wife's new allegiance to Jesus, may see Him as a threat to their marriage. A wife, jealous of her husband's newfound faith in Christ, may wonder where all this will lead. Parents whose teenagers embrace Christ may worry they will now lose their primary influence over their children. Perhaps their children will give to Jesus the obedience and love they feel only they should receive.

Herod felt threatened by Jesus. And Christmas can be a threat to our family, friends, and neighbors — a threat to their independence, their pride, and their ultimate destiny. Not everyone wants God to interrupt their world and their lives. Not everyone wants to bow down to God. They want to be their own god. Where we see the love of God in the Babe in the manger, they see Him grown up and making claims upon their lives, uncomfortable claims.

They have nothing to celebrate, even if the story is true. Especially if the story is true. They have said no to joy, to grace, to mercy, to peace — to the God who humbled Himself before them. And their goal is to steal our joy.

It is so easy to get angry with these people — especially when they are hostile and even cruel to us. They may be parents, family, spouses, friends, employees, or children. But to have the spirit of Christmas is to have the spirit of Christ, who loved even those who would reject Him. And in the true spirit of Christmas we must ask Christ to put His heart in us.

When we hear "bah-humbug" we shouldn't lash out or try to get even. We should be sensitive to the fact that they don't yet recognize that the Babe who was born in our world waits to be born in their hearts as well. We must model the spirit of Christ, the spirit of Christmas to them.

Can you remember when the message of Christmas meant little more to you than a holiday celebrated with trees and presents? Yet Jesus waited patiently until you learned that He had been born for you. As Martin Luther said, "Of what benefit would it be to me if Christ had been born a thousand times, and it would daily be sung into my ears in a most lovely manner, if I were never to hear that He was born for me and was to be my very own?"[6]

Grinches are afraid that Jesus has come to *take* something from them. We need to gently remind them that He came to *give* them something — something they can't live without.

Reflection and Celebration

Each year we join millions of other frantic and stressed-out Christmas shoppers in stores and malls. And many of these people—perhaps most—do not know their Savior. He remains a stranger to them. They may drink at the community well of celebration, yet it will not satisfy their thirst.

When you are standing in line at the checkout counter or pushing through crowds at the mall, it is very tempting to ignore those around you. Don't! Instead of lamenting the long line you are in, pick out someone in that line and silently pray for them. Ask Jesus to reveal Himself to them. Pray that, if they are not believers, the scales will fall from their eyes. See those around you with His eyes and allow yourself to feel their lostness. Don't just pray a general prayer—pray specifically, for specific people. Pray for the gruff old man, or the rebellious teenager, or the callous clerk. You may be the only one this Christmas who prays for them. You may be the only one who ever prays for them!

This year, pray for the Grinches and the Herods who surround you at Christmas. Give each of them the secret and precious Christmas gift of intercession on their behalf. Only in eternity will we know the effects of our stealth Christmas mission.

NINE

❄

March of the Once-Wooden Soldiers

Wooden soldiers are a popular Christmas decoration. They are celebrated in *The Nutcracker Suite*, in "The March of the Wooden Soldiers" in the operetta *Babes in Toyland*, and in other enchanting holiday stories. Gaily-colored wooden soldiers can be found hanging on Christmas trees, painted on storefront windows, or standing at attention on fireplace mantels. They can be thirty feet tall and fill the center of your favorite mall at Christmas time, or small enough to fit in the palm of your hand.

The quaint tale of a wooden soldier coming to life is endearing and magical. And while it is a firmly entrenched part of our cultural Christmas, it does not seem to have anything to do with the true meaning of Christmas. Admittedly, the origins of the wooden soldier story have nothing to do with the Christmas story itself. But the idea of wooden soldiers coming to life is to me an apt picture of what the entrance of God into our world began.

When God created man and woman in the Garden of Eden, He created them truly human. They did not know evil, and their thoughts and actions were perfect and completely in line with their Creator. They were without sin, without corruption—able to live in God's presence without guilt. However, when sin entered man's nature, our nature, we were no longer truly human the way God created us to be. Sin forever marred His original design.

When this occurred, we forfeited our true humanity and had to settle for what could accurately be termed a "wooden humanity." On the outside we looked human, but inside we had become wooden, lifeless, less than truly human. In essence, we traded in our true humanity for a wooden one.

Half of the Christmas miracle is the wonderful truth that God humbled Himself to become a man. The other half is the reason He did so: to make us sons of God. He came to help us rediscover what we had lost in the Garden. He lowered Himself in order to lift us up, sacrificing His perfect life in order to give us a new one. This is the reverse Christmas miracle.

The First Truly Human Baby

On that blessed Christmas morning over two thousand years ago, young Mary delivered the first truly human child. There was no wood in Him, for He was born without the sinful nature we had inherited from Adam and Eve. Mary's young arms cradled the first human who would perfectly fulfill the potential God had designed into the human race.

When Joseph and Mary, the shepherds, the Magi, and Simeon and Anna greeted the Christ child, they were each seeing true humanity for the first time. Each one of the main characters of our Christmas story had been born wooden, for they had lost their true humanity in the Garden. Woodenness was all they had ever known, in themselves or in anyone else. But here was a child who would be totally different from them in every way, yet share their same human nature and physical limitations.

Have you ever asked yourself what a perfect child acts like? Could you even imagine it? How does He respond to hunger, thirst, loneliness, cold, pain, or any other type of discomfort? I know as a parent how my three children responded to these experiences, but I have no idea how perfect humanity would respond. Yet Mary and Joseph experienced it.

How does a wooden soldier react to a real one? I can only wonder what it was like to look into eyes that reflected back only perfection. Each and every human response our Lord gave as a child, and then as a young man, was perfect. In a way it must have been terribly strange for Joseph and Mary and the family. How does someone who loves imperfectly parent a child who loves perfectly? At times their response to Him must have been less than adequate. He was what they could not hope to be. Perfect holiness was His birthright, as much a part of Him as His physical body.

We all know the experience of being in the presence of someone who is superior to us. Some of those individuals are humble and gracious and put us immediately at ease, never making us feel inadequate in any way. But others go out of their way to highlight our inadequacies. Subtly, or not so subtly, they use our deficiencies as an opportunity to brag or boast about themselves.

But this is not why God became a man. He did not become truly human in order to show us all up. His goal was not to shame us. Though we had lost our true humanity, God became a man to help us discover it again. He had not given up on His original plan. Though we had been wooden so long that we didn't even know what true humanity looked like, He came and reminded us. He became like us, and lived among us, to give us a divine boost. His very presence reminded us of what we were meant to be.

Even at Christmas, when our natures are on their best behavior, we can see our woodenness. We long to be truly unselfish, and we might be closer to that goal at Christmas than at any other time. But if we have given an expensive present to someone, we often expect to get one in return. When we don't, our feelings get hurt. We know we shouldn't feel that way, but we can't help it. When we receive an unexpected gift from someone we barely know, or from a casual business acquaintance, we feel indebted to return the favor. There is no love or true generosity in this act; it is strictly commercial. We are repaying an unspoken debt. Even when we can see the hypocrisy in the act, we go through with it.

Christ's birth was God's signal that He had come to change our woodenness into true humanity. He had no plans to populate His heaven with wooden soldiers. And this is one of the greatest truths of the Christmas season. When we place our faith in Him, He declares us to be sons of God, and then He slowly begins to make us real again.

We are odd creatures. We live with the dying remnants of the old wood within us, but also with the vibrant new humanity that has been planted in us by grace through faith. The Babe in the manger, who once came to live among us, now chooses to live within us, encouraging us, comforting us, and reminding us that we were reborn to be real.

Shedding the Dead Wood

Christmas lists. We make them every year. Lists of those who sent us Christmas cards last year. Lists of those to whom we should send cards this year. Lists of gifts we want to give to family and friends. Lists of gifts we want our family to get for us. I think long and hard about my gift list, because I want to give gifts that are truly desired or needed. But there are certain gifts we'd really like that no one can get for us. When my kids ask me what I want for Christmas, I don't tell them, "Well, what I'd really like is for your attitude to change, and for you to become more thoughtful to your sister and brother!" They can't wrap that up and give it to me. So, inevitably, I just ask for world peace and they roll their eyes and say, "Daaaad!"

What I would really like to receive is a Christmas gift that is labeled, "For Dan: Enclosed please find patience when you are tired and frustrated, trust when you are worried, understanding when you are unreasonable, and a double helping of unconditional love." I want to be a little less Dan and a little more a son of God. Less wood, more real humanity, that's my request.

For many years the only person I cared about was myself, and it showed. Patience was foreign to me, and forgiveness was a concept I never truly grasped. But when I allowed Jesus into my heart, He began a good work in me. What amazed me was how welcome the changes were in my life. I had no idea how fulfilling it would be to become truly human.

The first time I genuinely forgave someone from my heart was a milestone. I knew then that I had been irrevocably changed. I was no longer just going through the external motions, pretending to forgive but secretly harboring a grudge. I honestly, truly, and completely forgave the person. It was like the first small spring bud on a leafless tree—a sign that new life was indeed growing. I who was once wooden and dead was now coming fully alive.

When we find ourselves caring far more about someone else than we do about ourselves, we have shed our wooden nature and become, even for a brief time, truly human. Such selfless compassion is not a familiar feeling to us. It seems both natural and unnatural—but welcome. Part of our wooden heart is becoming real, and the transformation is strange, but delightful. It is like the moment when a child takes his first step or speaks for the first time. He is growing out of his childish immaturity, and those small, tantalizing victories whet his appetite for more. Yes, we frequently stumble in our new life, but surely walking can't be far away—and then running!

When our hearts begin to break for the lonely and helpless, we are shedding the wood of our old nature and experiencing more of the life the Christ child came to bring. When another person's happiness and peace become even more important to us than our own, we are fully immersed in the spirit of Christmas. When serving someone else brings us greater joy than being served, when we seek the limelight for others rather than for ourselves, when delighting our heavenly Father becomes our greatest passion, we are shedding our wood.

Christmas is one of our greatest celebrations for many reasons, not least of which is the reality that God is making us into different people. Day by day, month by month, year by year we are shedding a little more of the woodenness of our old natures and becoming more like the sons and daughters of God that we are. Sons and daughters of God! What a concept. To think that I am a son of God right now fills me with such gratitude and joy — more gratitude and joy than can be expressed in all the Christmas music ever written. I'm a son now — not when I die and go to heaven, but right now. He became like me 2000 years ago so that I could become more like Him today.

It is, of course, only fitting that at Christmas we celebrate His incarnation. But it is equally fitting that we celebrate our transformation from wooden soldiers back into human beings.

Taking the Right Cues

Admittedly, many people temporarily change their behavior at Christmas time. Even those who do not know or acknowledge the Savior seem more cheerful or display more compassion and generosity. But they take their cues strictly from the season itself, much as a scoffer knows enough to snuff out his cigarette and watch his language when entering the church. Those who have become sons and daughters of God take their cues from the Babe in the manger who has been born into their hearts.

As Madeleine L'Engle wrote, "Christ, the Second Person of the Trinity, Christ, the Maker of the universe or perhaps many universes, willingly and lovingly leaving all that power and coming to this poor, sin-filled planet to live with us for a few years to show us what we ought to be and could be. Christ came to us as Jesus of Nazareth, wholly human and wholly divine, to show us what it means to be made in God's image."[1]

We have been awakened from our wooden slumber. We are now becoming truly human. We are not perfect; there is still much of the wooden about us. But that will always be true in this life. What is amazing is that there is any of the truly human in us at all—that God has begun to bring us to life here and now.

Every tender thought, every kind word, every act of mercy and grace, every offer of forgiveness, patience, and under-standing celebrates the reverse Christmas miracle of our Great Awakening, which began when the first real human came to earth and showed us what it means to be real.

The march of the once-wooden soldiers has begun.

Reflection and Celebration

If your Christmas decorations don't include a wooden soldier, consider buying one this Christmas. If you already have one, take it out and dust it off. Put it in a place where you'll see it often—maybe at work on your desk, or in your car if you travel a great deal. No one can object to this seemingly generic Christmas decoration.

Each time you look at this wooden soldier, remember that you were once wooden but are now becoming truly human. Remember how you are being changed. You are a son or daughter of God. And when you become aware of some of your lingering wooden traits like anger, jealousy, envy, and sensuality rising to the surface, ask God to forgive you and help you remember that He came to save you from your woodenness.

Many of us write a Christmas letter each year to family and friends, celebrating the past year and all it has brought to our lives. We thank God for His many blessings to us—material, physical, and emotional. This year, how about writing your own private letter to God, thanking Him that you are becoming more truly human? Thank Him for ways He has done this specifically for you this past year. Thank Him most for the changes of heart you have experienced, for this is where you are becoming most truly human—for the ability to forgive, to understand, to empathize, to be patient, to be unselfish. You won't have achieved perfection in any of these areas, but it is important to note the progress God is making in your heart.

Truly human, that is what Jesus was—and what we're being transformed into. Join the parade!

TEN

❄

One More Gift
To Give

She had seemingly done everything possible to destroy her relationship with her husband and ruin her life. When they married, she had promised to be a faithful and devoted wife, because, quite honestly, no one had ever treated her as well as he had. She would have been a fool to think of chasing other lovers; in fact the thought didn't enter her mind.

Besides, she wasn't particularly attractive or winsome. Other women were definitely more striking and popular. And she had several obvious character flaws, was frequently ungrateful, dishonest, and a terrible complainer. Yet this man had looked past all her shortcomings and chosen her—and treated her like a queen.

Unfortunately, her character flaws slowly destroyed their relationship. The more her husband demonstrated his love and concern for her, the more she took it for granted. Eventually she even grew tired of his devotion and began to flirt with other men. Only a little at first, though she knew it hurt her husband. But eventually she became blatant and unrepentant about her affairs.

In spite of all this, her husband begged and pleaded for her to return and be faithful to him, warning her that these dalliances were ruining their relationship and would destroy her life forever. But by that time her love for him had grown cold. His words no longer had any effect on her. So finally, with a heavy heart, he said "enough," and let her go.

With all marital restraints removed she chased after many lovers and became involved in their dangerous and sordid lifestyles. This soon took its toll on her, and she became terribly sick. But her lovers didn't care; they were sick themselves. She grew hard and callous, and the weight of all her mistakes burdened her beyond hope.

All was very, very dark. Everything her husband had predicted had come true. She prepared to slide away into bitter oblivion.

Then, at her lowest point of despair, an unexpected ray of sunlight pierced the gloom—a message from her husband. Though she had spurned, humiliated, betrayed, and abandoned him, he reached out to her once more with a promise of forgiveness, hope, acceptance, and love. A promise of a tomorrow that would make her forget all her horrible failures and yesterdays.

Today, we hear some of the words of that faithful husband to his unfaithful wife repeated thousands of times every Christmas season: "For to us a child is born, to us a son is given, and the government will be on his shoulders. And he will be called Wonderful Counselor, Mighty God, Everlasting Father, Prince of Peace" (Isaiah 9:6).

Are you surprised? Does this popular Christmas text seem new to you now? I hope so. Because only when we see this verse and promise in its original context do we begin to understand its awesome significance. For Israel is the unfaithful wife, as are you and I. God is the faithful husband who, in the middle of a passage detailing judgment to come upon Israel, pauses to express His love to His beloved bride one more time and offers a promise out of love, not obligation. The above passage is the fulfillment of God's promise to give us a gift that would heal our broken relationship with Him. The day our Lord was born, this hopeful and long-forgotten promise was fulfilled.

Sin creates distance in any relationship, but the greatest distance it creates is between God and us. Something had to bridge that gulf and bring our faithless hearts back to Him. That something was the Son—the presence of the Son with us.

There is power in presence. Steve Brown, in his book *Overcoming Setbacks*, relates a true story that gives a clear picture of this.

"A young wife and mother, overwhelmed by her responsibilities, walked out on her family one day. She just laid down her apron and left. When she called that night, her frantic husband demanded an explanation. But she just hung up. She called every week to check on the children, but she refused to let them know where she was. The husband pleaded with her to return, but she wouldn't listen. Finally, he tracked her down to a dumpy hotel on the other side of the state. When she answered the door, he poured out his love for her and begged her to come home. She fell into his arms and cried for forgiveness. Later, when her husband asked why she hadn't returned before, she replied, 'All those claims of love—they were just words before. But then you came.'"[1]

"But then you came." There is power in the loved ones presence and at the manger, God gave us the gift of His presence. Even though we didn't deserve it, God sent a child to be born to us and seek us out. The Christmas spirit is fueled in us when we celebrate the fulfillment of this promise from the God who loved us in spite of our personal failures.

So let's revisit this famous passage that adorns countless Christmas cards and is quoted from thousands of pulpits, taking time to meditate upon each unique aspect of this miraculous sign.

"a child is born"

*I*saiah is in the midst of prophesying against Israel because of her unfaithfulness. Very soon he will tell the Israelites that the Assyrians will be God's instrument of discipline, coming down upon Israel and overwhelming her. Yet God interrupts this tragic prophecy to speak tenderly about Israel's future, promising that He will never abandon her, despite her unfaithfulness. As evidence of this promise, a child will be born to her.

"Therefore the Lord himself will give you a sign: The virgin will be with child and will give birth to a son, and will call him Immanuel" (Isaiah 7:14).

This not an allegorical lesson or a comforting thought that amounts to no more than wishful thinking. No, this is a real promise. God would someday deliver His wayward bride, and that deliverance would involve a miraculous human birth at a definite time and place in history.

Has anyone ever made a vague promise to you — something upon which you placed great hope, only to learn later that the person hadn't meant for you to take his words so seriously? Have *you* ever made a vague promise you meant to keep, but didn't? We all do this: parents to children, children to parents, friend to friend, relative to relative. We promise to visit, to help, to show up, but for one reason or another, we never do it.

When we make promises we really intend to keep, we get specific with dates, times, and details. And that's what God did with Israel. He got specific about this coming Messiah. This wouldn't be just any child; it would be a child born of a virgin. That is specific with an exclamation mark!

But notice, this same child would not only be born *to a virgin*, He would also be born *to us*. This child would be born to Israel. And all who have become children of Abraham by faith also benefit from God's eternal plan. This child was a gift not simply to Israel, but to all of mankind.

Then Isaiah gets even more specific. This child will be *born of a virgin*, will be *born to us*, and will *be a son*.

"a son is given"

One day in eternity the Father spoke to the Son about His plan for His creation. In response, the Son disguised His glorious divinity, descended to earth, and under the cloak of humanity became the promised child. A child was *born*; the Son was *given*.

Mary birthed Jesus, but not until after the Father had first given Him. He was the Son from all eternity, but on a given day He became a child. This was to identify this special child with His eternal, divine origins.

The tradition of gift giving in which we participate so fervently and eagerly at this season can be traced ultimately to the Father. The giving began with Him. The greatest gifts came from Him. He gave us a world to live in, and He gave us life to enjoy it. Then, when through our own sin we forfeited that life, the Father gave again. He gave us His Son, and through Him new life, eternal life, not merely as His creation, but as His beloved children.

That life, however, came with a price tag we couldn't afford. Like the expensive car that is way out of our reach, or the house we could never afford to even think about buying. We did not deserve this second chance, so it had to be given.

"and the government will be on his shoulders"

People look to their governmental leaders to provide prosperity, peace, justice, compassion, and guidance. But the governments of the world have rested on some pretty weak and narrow shoulders over the years, and none have ever measured up to this lofty goal. In fact, precious few have even sought such a self-sacrificial end. Most seek only their own power and self-aggrandizement.

We tend to be hard on our leaders when they fail, but we must remember that they have an inherent handicap. They are imperfect, sinful human beings. We might as well ask a cow to fly south for the winter, or a dog to live underwater like a fish, as ask an imperfect person to govern perfectly.

Imperfect people make imperfect laws, which they imperfectly enforce, and which are ultimately powerless to change imperfect hearts. In the days of the French Revolution, when the citizens of France sought to overthrow a tyrannous monarchy, a fiery soldier named Napoleon Bonaparte championed the cause of the revolution and the free man's republic. He became the French people's hero, helping to draft just laws and rebuild fractured France into a mighty power. Then he did something completely human: he crowned himself emperor for life. The very man who had offered his country such hope and promise now brought great suffering through his own tyranny. He could conquer armies, but not his own weaknesses.

Imagine a government that would be perfect, righteous, fair, effective, and compassionate. Wouldn't that be wonderful? But who would be qualified to lead such a government? Who could bear such a burden? Only the Child born to us, the Son given to us. Because one day the government of all nations and all people *will* be given to Him forever, and He will govern perfectly, righteously, and eternally.

"and he will be called Wonderful Counselor"

*L*ife is full of so many choices, so many decisions that need to be made. Often we seek counselors who can help us make the right ones. But every counselor is himself in need of a counselor. Because, try as we might, it is impossible for any of us imperfect human beings to have a perfect perspective. None of us have all the answers, all the time. Wouldn't it be just, well — *wonderful* if we did?

Isaiah's use of the Hebrew word *pele*, meaning "wonder," indicates that everything about Jesus is a wonder. He is extraordinarily beyond all we could ever imagine. Jesus is such a wonder, so perfectly capable, that He has no need of counselors. He never has to ask advice, or "get back" to us on something. He has all the answers to everything all the time. Isn't that wonderful?

As a pastor, I also must be a counselor; this is a role to which God has called me. But even doing my best, it is impossible for me to counsel perfectly. I look back on some of the counsel I gave fifteen years ago and cringe. I meant well, but I lacked maturity or perspective or all the necessary information. Most importantly, I lacked a perfect heart and mind.

The perfect heart and mind are blended in God's gift to us of a Wonderful Counselor.

"Mighty God"

In the Hebrew, *El Gibbor* is translated "God, the mighty one." However, the word *Gibbor* actually means "hero." It could be translated "a heroic God," or "a God of a hero" — a hero whose chief quality is that He is God. He is not just our God; He is our hero. For He not only has the *power*, but also the *desire* to rescue us.

Notice the contrast between the terms *Mighty God*, *child*, and *Son*. We think of God's Son as the meek and gentle child Jesus. But remember, He was in disguise. He was God cloaked in humanity. God incognito. From everlasting, the child born, the Son given, was and is *El Gibbor*, the Mighty God.

We've already talked about people who make promises they don't intend to keep. But what about the person who can't deliver on his promise because he doesn't have the power to make it happen? Is there anything more disappointing? Yet all of the promises implied by these titles of the coming Christ child would be fulfilled because He would be *El Gibbor*, the Mighty God.

"Everlasting Father"

In this phrase, Isaiah is not confusing Jesus the Son with God the Father. Instead, Isaiah is describing the nature of the Messiah's relationship with His people and His relationship with time. This child to be born is eternal, and He is fatherly in His dealings with us.

Father! The very word is a catalyst, evoking strong emotions. We love our fathers; we blast our fathers. We blame them for our condition; we bless them for our condition. But whether we bless them or blast them, we all seem to be looking and longing for that perfect father relationship. But our fathers are temporary and imperfect, even the best of them. We yearn for One who will look out for us, protect us, provide for us, hold us in His strong arms, and answer all our dumb questions.

Whatever our minds and hearts can desire or imagine in a perfect Father, Jesus will be for us ... *forever*!

"Prince of Peace"

Almost the moment we are born, the conflicts begin. We fight with our parents, our siblings, our friends, our spouses, our children, our relatives, and our leaders. Peace is the eternally elusive pursuit of man. Peace between nations, peace between neighbors, peace between spouses, peace between family members, even peace in our own minds and hearts. Many men and women have achieved great things, but no one can claim to have brought the world real peace.

We want peace, but we also want our own way. We desire peace, but we can't remove all the peace-disturbing things in our life. I can feel at peace toward you, but what happens if you don't feel at peace toward me? A true and lasting peace in our world is simply beyond our reach. How appropriate that, then, as the names of Messiah are listed, the last one we hear echoing in our minds is Prince of Peace.

Peace is more than the absence of war, conflict, stress, or turmoil. To achieve true peace, we have to remove the ultimate cause of all these things, which is sin. Sin destroys both our personal peace and the peace of this world.

Sin was a ticking time bomb. In a very deliberate operation, Jesus absorbed the full blast of the sin explosion on the cross. He forever bears the scars of that explosion on His hands and feet.

Real lasting peace, for nations or individuals, is not something we achieve; it is something we receive through the Son. It is part of the gift.

Vance Havner once wrote, "Christmas is based on an exchange of gifts: the gift of God to man—His Son; and the gift of man to God—when we first give ourselves to God."[2] He gives Himself to us daily, moment by moment. And we give ourselves to Him not just once, at conversion, but a hundred times a day.

The true Christmas spirit reminds us again of His gift and of the proper response to that gift. He gives, and we give back. What can we give that would be appropriate for such a gift as His? Gratitude. It seems so small, and yet there is nothing greater we can give. To simply take time from our busy schedules and remember this tremendous gift He gave to us and to be overwhelmed all over again by His love. Tears of gratitude are pearls and diamonds we can offer Him, more precious to Him than all the money in the world.

He will forever be the child born to us, the Son given to us, the perfect governor, our Wonderful Counselor, our Mighty God, our Everlasting Father, our Prince of Peace.

Reflection and Celebration

As we have seen, Isaiah 9:6 is a promise of love and forgiveness to a nation and a people totally undeserving of it. It is a promise of forgiveness given in spite of, not because of, their (our) actions. It is a gift of love that is so far beyond human love, reason, and patience that it must be divine.

Each of us have people in our lives who have so hurt us, so humiliated us, or so angered us that we can hardly bear the mention of their names. Because of this, they have become non-persons in our lives—people we have chosen to ignore or forget. Yet we cannot forget that the wonderful promise of forgiveness and love in Isaiah 9:6 came to a people (us) who had hurt and offended God in every way possible. How can we who been shown such grace and mercy and love and forgiveness refuse it to others?

Since bitterness and the Christmas spirit cannot co-exist, ask Jesus to help you love the non-persons in your life. Take a moment to write down the names of those you have written out of your life. Now, as you remember their offenses against you, weigh those against the offenses you have committed against God. Focus not on their offenses against you, but how God forgives your offenses against Him. What Christmas brings us is perspective: the needed perspective of God's heart toward us, which reminds us of what our heart should be toward others — even those who have hurt us.

Ask God to strengthen you, help you, and guide you in how to forgive, to love, to truly wish someone well whom you would rather just forget. When you do this, the spirit of Christmas—the Spirit of Christ—has entered your life.

ELEVEN

❄

When It Doesn't Feel Like Christmas

*S*everal years ago I resigned from my pastorate of thirteen years to begin a new ministry. It was December and our house had recently sold, but the home we were moving into wasn't yet available. My sister, Keri, and brother-in-law, Phil, invited us to spend Christmas with them and stay until our house was ready at the end of the month. So we moved into their house in December, all six of us! My wife and I inhabited a tiny tent trailer set up in the garage, while my mother and our three kids slept in bedrooms no longer used by my sister's sons.

Phil and Keri's oldest son, Danny, was away in the Coast Guard. Their youngest son, Brian, had drowned a year earlier at the age of eighteen in a swimming accident at the local high school. The pain was still raw and tender, and Christmas simply accentuated their pain. All the sweet memories of Christmas with their sons were now tinged with the pain of Brian's death and Danny's absence. The sweet blissful holidays they had known for so long were now replaced by an ache that would not subside. My sister's family had lived only ten homes down from us for many years, and my kids had grown up with Brian, so his absence also saddened them greatly.

Christmas had always been my sister's favorite season, and each year our entire extended family celebrated Christmas Eve dinner at Phil and Keri's. Decorating was a passion with Keri, and each year her house glowed. From the tree, to the mantelpiece, to the many Christmas globes that Phil had collected over the years, their house radiated a quiet, quaint Christmas warmth.

But not this year. This year everything was different. Our own Christmas decorations were packed away in storage, and Phil and Keri simply couldn't bear to look at theirs. Each decoration was tinged with bittersweet memories. So the house was largely undecorated, mirroring all our hearts. No baubles of the holiday season could brighten our sad hearts. It was a strange Christmas; in fact it didn't feel like Christmas at all. Nothing was normal; nothing was comfortable; nothing was familiar.

My family was experiencing a difficult transition as well. Our children were adjusting to moving away from the only home and the only friends they had ever known to a strange town three hours away. Not being able to spend one last Christmas in our old house was painful for them. We were between two worlds, one familiar and comfortable, one foreign and frightening. We knew we could never go back, and yet we couldn't really go forward.

Memories of Brian filled our hearts and minds, and our loss was palpable. We tried hard to cheer each other up, but we knew that Christmas was never going to be the same. I remember feeling the same way when our grandmother died many years earlier. Memories of Christmas at Grandma's house were some of the best memories of my youth. And I had been right. Though we had eventually gotten over that loss, Christmas was never the same again.

We would never have Brian for another Christmas. We would never spend another Christmas in our old home. Few things are more painful than the realization that treasured moments with certain family and friends are now a thing of the past.

Painful Transitions and Losses

hristmas, for many, can be a time of opening raw wounds. When you are single, the family celebrations of Christmas can accentuate your aloneness. When a loved one is gone or when a family has been broken, Christmas can be a painful reminder of what has been lost.

Dr. Thomas Tewell tells the true story of a Christmas Eve service at Fifth Avenue Presbyterian Church in New York City. Among those who had gathered was a recovering alcoholic named Jim, six months sober. This was his first Christmas since having lost his family. A family of four sat two rows in front of him. Seeing them together reminded him of what he had lost, of what could have been his had his drinking not destroyed his family. Overwhelmed with sadness, he decided he just couldn't handle these feelings without a drink.

As he moved from the sanctuary to the narthex, he encountered Pastor Tewell. "Jim, where are you going?" Pastor Tewell asked.

"Oh, I'm just going out for a scotch," Jim replied.

"Jim, you can't do that," the pastor responded, knowing Jim was a recovering alcoholic. "Is your sponsor available?"

"It's Christmas Eve. My sponsor is in Minnesota. There's nobody who can help me. I just came tonight for a word of hope, and I ended up sitting behind this family. If I had my life together, I'd be here with my wife and kids, too."

Pastor Tewell took Jim into the vestry to talk with a couple of other pastors. Then he slipped into the sanctuary and before speaking to the congregation, he whispered a prayer: "O God, could you give me a word of hope for Jim?"

After welcoming those who had come to the service that evening and telling them about the church, he said, "I have one final announcement. If anyone here tonight is a friend of Bill Wilson—and if you are, you'll know it—could you step out for a moment and meet me in the vestry?" (Bill Wilson, better known as Bill W., is a cofounder of Alcoholics Anonymous.)

From all over the sanctuary, women, men, and college students stood up and made their way to the vestry. "And there while I was preaching in the sanctuary about incarnation," said Pastor Tewell, "the Word was becoming flesh in the vestry. Someone was experiencing hope."[1]

Missing the Traditional Trappings

In a strange and sadly ironic way, while the message of Christmas is about hope, the season itself prompts hopelessness in many. When you are used to an extravagant

Christmas with food, presents, and parties and you suddenly experience a reversal of fortune, Christmas is a reminder of what you have lost. You compare your present Christmas with the sweet memories of the past, and the result is sadness and depression.

Some, of course, have never experienced the warmth and familiar comfort of a traditional Christmas. It is totally foreign to them. They were never considered important or loved. No one ever tried to make Christmas special for them. And for some, Christmas was never even celebrated or acknowledged.

What Jim and many others find themselves missing is the traditional trappings of Christmas—family, togetherness, home, and familiarity. Culturally, in the West, Christmas has become a family celebration. But Christmas means far more than that. Christ did not enter our world so that we might have a comfortable, warm holiday celebration on planet Earth.

Each culture has its own traditions surrounding Christmas. While many of these traditions have little to do with the divine truth of God entering our world, they have become so inextricably intertwined with our Christmas celebrations that it is difficult, if not impossible, for us to separate the religious truth of Christmas from the human traditions we have grown up with. Therefore, when the painful reality of life interrupts our cultural celebrations of the Christmas season, when we lose some of those cultural supports, we believe we cannot experience the spirit of Christmas. For years the Christmas spirit has meant an immersion in the festal garb of the season, the colors, lights, decorations, songs, presents, family get-togethers—and yes, the story of the Babe in the manger.

But the Christmas story, the real story, has become a side-light to our celebration. It is important, but not absolutely essential. We could actually get through the season with great joy, celebration, and treasured memories without seriously considering the implications of the entrance of God into our world. A simple nod to "the reason behind the season" would suffice—even a brief one. Millions of Christians do it every year and appear none the worse for it.

Something Different, Something Deeper

*B*ut what happens when a broken family or the aching emptiness caused by the loss of a loved one or unexpected catastrophe or financial loss or the deterioration of our health or fragmented and painful relationships conspire to challenge the Christmas message of "good news of a great joy"? No Christmas carol can fill our broken hearts with joy; no amount of decorations and presents can make up for what we have lost. The twinkling lights and festive atmosphere can no longer work their magic on us.

What we need is something different, something deeper. But we've celebrated Christmas the same way for so long we aren't sure there is anything different, anything deeper. Our Christmas crutches have been removed and our worship legs are atrophied. Never before has it taken so much effort to celebrate Christmas, if indeed we can find in our hearts any motivation to try. Christmas has become a cruel reminder of our trouble rather than a poignant reminder of our hope.

It is in these moments that we begin to see how far we have strayed from the true message of this blessed season. Most of the festal aspects of Christmas that have come to define the season for so many of us are only a few hundred years old. Yet Christmas has been celebrated for over two thousand years. Brennan Manning, in his book *Lion and Lamb: The Relentless Tenderness of Jesus*, asks, "Do you think you could contain Niagara Falls in a teacup? Is there anyone in our midst who pretends to understand the awesome love in the heart of Abba of Jesus that inspired, motivated and brought about Christmas? The shipwrecked at the stable kneel in the presence of mystery."[2]

Unless we dwell upon this mystery, letting it take center stage, we will chase the true spirit of Christmas to no avail. This is the Christmas message that crosses all cultural boundaries.

Author and speaker Jill Briscoe recalls being asked to speak to a church gathering in Croatia for two hundred newly arrived refugees. They were mostly women, because the men were either dead, or in camp, or fighting. She was scheduled to speak in the evening, but after seeing their terrible situation, what she had prepared seemed totally inadequate. So she put her notes away and prayed, "God, give me creative ideas they can identify with." That evening she told the refugees about Jesus, who as a baby became a refugee Himself. He was hunted by soldiers, and His parents had to flee to Egypt at night, leaving everything behind. Sensing that her audience was listening intently, she continued telling them about Jesus' life, and when she got to the cross, she said, "He hung there naked, not like the pictures tell you." Her listeners knew what that meant. Some of them had been stripped naked and tortured. At the end of the message, she said, "All these things have happened to you. You are homeless. You have had to flee. You have suffered unjustly. But you didn't have a choice. He had a choice. He knew all this would happen to Him, but He still came." Then she told them why. Many of the refugees knelt down, put their hands up, and wept. "He's the only one who really understands," she concluded. "How can I possibly understand, but He can."[3]

This is the part of the Christmas story that we have often neglected. God had a choice, and that choice carried serious and deadly consequences. It began with Him abandoning His divine glory and humiliating Himself, making Himself as vulnerable as Deity could make Himself, becoming a human child. He came to suffer and die. There is no tragedy, humiliation, loss, or pain that He has not known. We can festively decorate the message of His entrance into our world with mangers, angels, stars, wise men, and shepherds. But we cannot festively decorate the purpose of His entrance.

Pain — Part of the Christmas Spirit

*I*ronically, in those times when it least feels like Christmas, it might *be* most like Christmas. When nothing seems comfortable, or normal, or familiar, we are closer to experiencing the purpose of Christmas than at any other time. We are nearer the true Christmas spirit than we could ever imagine.

Our Lord must have been uncomfortable when He left everything that was eternally familiar and took on human nature. He who had known only glory and absolute perfection suddenly found Himself living among sinners in a fallen world. There was nothing comfortable, normal, or familiar about the incarnation for our Lord. This move was not a step up for Him; it was an infinite leap down. Yet, this was Christmas.

Mary, like any normal young woman, must have had dreams of what her marriage to Joseph and their life together would be like. Then came the angelic visitation. Yes, she was the blessed one, the mother of our Lord. The angelic visitation and the divine honor bestowed on her were nothing short of incredible. But that is the heavenly perspective. From all earthly viewpoints she had been unfaithful to her betrothed husband, Joseph, who was too good a man to divorce her. Normalcy for Mary was but a distant memory from the moment of her supernatural conception on. Who could identify with her pain? Who could understand, really? Who would quiet the gossip, the speculation, the finger-pointing?

When Mary discovered that Herod had murdered all the male babies in Bethlehem, trying to destroy her special child, how do you think she felt? Mary and Joseph were far from family and familiarity and any kind of comfort zone. Somehow the words "Merry Christmas" just don't fit their experience.

Yet, the angels rejoiced! And Mary proclaimed that God had blessed her, extolling His mercy (Luke 1:46–56). Immanuel was coming. God was visiting our planet!

Everything about the true story of Christmas points us to a God who cares about us far more than we can ever understand. He left perfection and peace to enter chaos on a divine rescue mission, bringing us salvation and hope.

Life isn't perfect—and it never will be until He comes again to make all things right. But this isn't the end of the story. Our heavenly visitor reminds us that another, far greater world exists. Our God not only left His world to enter ours so we would know He loves us, but so that He could make us ready for our new home—our eternal home.

Maybe hope, in the midst of strange, uncomfortable, and confusing circumstances, is the closest we can get to the true and original spirit of Christmas. Often, the lack of the internal peace we are seeking so desperately conspires to convince us that God's love for us—us personally—has waned. How can God truly love us when He allows such pain and suffering to enter our lives? How can we worship God's love in a season that accentuates our greatest pain? But it was because of this very pain and suffering that God came in the first place.

The Christmas Unpeace

*I*n fact, it was into just such "unpeace" that our Lord arrived. As author Emmy Arnold writes, "How could God hate us, when He gives us what He, past all measure, loves? I proclaim to you great joy that shall come to all peoples—peace on earth! The true Christmas experience is to feel that this Christmas peace is the greater power; that even now on earth it overcomes all unpeace. That this peace shall come to all—that is the expectation and faith of Christmas. The Christmas Star in the night sky, the shining of the Christmas light in the night—all this is the sign that light breaks into the darkness. Though we see about us the darkness of unrest, of family discord, of class struggle, of competitive jealousy and of national hatred, the light shall shine and drive it out. Wherever the Christmas Child is born in a heart, wherever Jesus begins His earthly life anew—that is where the life of God's love and of God's peace dawns again."[4]

When all those things that spell security and comfort are removed, we become keenly aware of how much we needed God to enter our world. We can't make heaven on earth, no matter how hard we try, no matter how much we decorate. Sin has affected and infected everything we touch. We needed to be rescued. We needed a Savior.

And we long for peace. Peace on earth, and peace in our hearts. This is what the original participants in the Christmas story were waiting and hoping for.

A powerful way to appreciate having a Savior is to imagine what it would be like not to have one. Imagine that your pain and suffering have no real meaning. Your short life is simply ruled by fate—and you are just unlucky. Wrongs will never be made right, truth is relative, and hope for a better world is just so much dreaming. Your silent suffering and hidden pain have no divine audience; they are yours to bear alone. There exists, quite simply, no hope beyond this life.

But we do have reason for rejoicing. A Savior *was* born to us, and our suffering touches His merciful and gracious heart. He was not only moved by our suffering; He came to join us in it. He lowered Himself to suffer what we suffer, to feel what we feel, to cry with us, hunger with us, thirst with us, and live with us. The almighty God made Himself vulnerable to all the pain of human life. And to keep us from eternal suffering, He came to die for us, taking our place.

One of my greatest joys is in knowing that there is a God and that He is righteous and loving. My Savior is absolute truth, utterly pure of heart, perfect in mind, infinite in knowledge, undiluted holiness, untainted and eternally unchangeable in His nature. That this God loves me never ceases to amaze me. So my hope can shine through any pain, confusion, and suffering that comes my way, because I know my Savior cares for me. He who records each of my tears (Psalm 56:8) came to love me to death. My hope cannot be quenched, because I know my God loves me even through suffering.

Christmas reminds us that we can put our hope in a sure thing—the love of God—demonstrated so beautifully on that wonderful day when He came forth into our world as a babe. Because of our despair, hopelessness, and helplessness He left His throne in heaven. This is the "good news of great joy that will be for all the people" (Luke 2:10). This is the Christmas we can all celebrate, with or without family, friends, or familiarity. This spirit of Christmas goes beyond trees, decorations, songs, and presents to speak to our true condition. And to this we can honestly say, "Merry Christmas."

Reflection and Celebration

Our life circumstances seem ever changing. Sometimes that means we are removed from all that is familiar. When that happens, Christmas can seem strange, sad, and a painful reminder of what we have lost.

Instead of slipping into despair this season because your circumstances have changed for the worse, realize that what you are experiencing is a real part of the Christmas story. Go back and re-read the story with an eye to seeing how different and uncomfortable the first Christmas was for Mary and Joseph. Anyone can celebrate success, prosperity, and comfort. You have the opportunity to display a true Christmas spirit of acceptance and submission to your present circumstances

Remember God's love displayed for you already. Remember that He knows your sufferings and joins you in them. If your life is truly blessed and comfortable this year, seek out someone who is going through difficult or even tragic circumstances, perhaps divorce or separation, sickness or financial difficulties, or some other trial. Send them a letter, give them a call, pray for them, and in this way display the spirit of compassion that Christmas calls forth in us.

Set aside some of your "Christmas time" to spend with someone you know is hurting or suffering in some way during this season. If they are suffering too deeply to join your celebration of Christmas, perhaps you could meet together for dessert or coffee to dispense to them a special measure of Christ's love through you.

TWELVE

✻

The Magi's Surprise

*E*very Christmas we hear again the timeless melodies that celebrate our Savior's birth. Each one, in its own way, points to that amazing event. One of the most popular is a song so familiar that it has become embedded in our culture.

We three kings of Orient are
Bearing gifts, we traverse afar —
Field and fountain, moor and mountain,
Following yonder star.

The visit of the Wise Men, or the Magi as the Bible calls them, is celebrated every Christmas with great pomp and circumstance in churches all around the world. These splendidly garbed visitors coming to find the king of the Jews, guided by a star, journeying a great distance, have become such a familiar part of our pageantry that we usually don't think about the difficulties or the deeper meaning of their journey (Matthew 2:1–12). So while the ancient story scarcely needs retelling, it desperately needs revisiting.

The Magi were searching for the newborn king of the Jews. They didn't know who He really was; they just knew that He was, in some way, very special.

Our world is filled with people attracted to Jesus, yet unsure of who He really is. They, like the Magi, have some information about Him, but not enough. Furthermore, not everything they have been told is true.

This is especially the case with those who did not grow up in church and Sunday school. Their images of Jesus are largely gleaned from popular culture, religious leaders, and mass media. For the most part, Jesus is a curiosity to them — a man both worshiped and cursed, adored and reviled.

A number of years ago our local paper ran an article on Christmas morning entitled, "Who Say Ye That I Am?" The newspaper had asked historians and theologians from many "traditions" to reflect on Jesus and His birth. One minister said, "The place we will find Jesus is not in a manger in Bethlehem, but in recognizing Christ in the people we meet." When I read that, I couldn't help thinking, "Just try finding Jesus in some of the people I've met and you'd give up the search."

Swami Viprananda said, "Jesus is the reincarnation of God who had a divine mission to bring to humanity an understanding of its true nature — that we are all divine." So God sent Jesus to earth to tell us that we are all divine? If we were divine, why was He in heaven and we on earth? Besides, if we were really divine, wouldn't we figure it out on our own?

The local rabbi said that Jesus was "a teacher, a decent person, and a Jew." This is the popular Jewish position, so no surprise there. The Unitarian minister said the "virgin birth is a metaphor for the purity of children and the love of parents and the sense of awe at creation." In other words, it's just make-believe, a story with a good moral, on a par with the film *It's a Wonderful Life!* The Buddhist minister had an interesting take. Ignoring Jesus' amazing birth, he referred to the thirty or so missing years of Jesus' life history, suggesting that, according to legend, Jesus spent those lost years in Tibet studying with monks and going by the name Issa. *Please.*

A professor of religion at Chapman University, commenting on the Christmas story, posited this idea: "Could it be that the story of Christmas that takes us beyond the pleasant 'legends' of the wise men, angels, and shepherds is that of an outcast mother and her illegitimate birth?" So a professor of religion holds the view that Jesus was just another illegitimate baby, and all the rest is just "legend."[1]

We who have grown up with the Christmas story sometimes have a hard time relating to those who are searching. We hear one truth; they hear many interpretations and opinions. We know one Jesus; they are offered dozens. We forget what it's like to be a seeker. The wonderful story that prompts joy and worship in us prompts confusion in them.

Yet, like the Magi, many people who go looking for Jesus find far more than they expect. And, like the Magi, many more discover that they cannot find Him without His help. God uses different means to ignite our search for Him. With the Magi it was a star. With the shepherds it was angels. Ah, the wisdom of God. He adjusts His methods to our peculiar personality, adjusting and catering to our uniqueness, and even to our weakness.

God Led Them in a Way They Would Understand

While the exact identity of the Magi is impossible to determine, we do know that they were considered men of science, learning, and religion, and that they depended upon astrology to ascertain movements in time and history. They weren't hawking horoscopes for the locals; they were serious men seeking truth the only way they knew how.

Since the Magi were astronomers, studying the wonders of the heavens, God led these men through astronomical phenomena. Their eyes were focused on the stars, so that's what He used to get their attention. And though they were serious scientists, they also certainly had a bit of the astrologer in them.

The ancients regarded the appearance of a new star or comet as an omen of some remarkable event or birth. While the Bible condemns the practice of astrology, God guided the Magi in a way familiar to them. Do we find this strange? We shouldn't. No one knows us better than God. He knew what it would take to get the Magi's attention.

God meets us where we are and uses means we understand to draw us toward Him. Those who demand intellectual evidence will find the path to Him strewn with logic, brilliance, and reason. Every scene in nature is imprinted with His omniscient design. Many have followed the amazing complexity of our world and been led to the creator Himself.

Others seek someone who will meet their emotional needs. Here again God humbles Himself before us, showing Himself to be a tender and attentive heavenly Father, lavishly displaying His love in ways we can understand—offering forgiveness, comfort, friendship, and unconditional love.

Still others seek to find Jesus because He alone can bring change into their lives, and change is their greatest need. So He has left a paper trail, detailing the amazing metamorphosis of eleven disciples—timid, fearful men who later became giants, leaders, and willing martyrs. He also gives us countless modern-day examples of His power to change people.

But at the beginning of the story, the Magi followed the stars, and God revealed Himself to them in a way they would understand. Not fully, of course. They could not fully understand the person of Christ through the star alone. But He could prompt them to begin the search by creating a celestial anomaly that would arouse their curiosity.

One of the great surprises in the search for Jesus is the revelation that the One we have been looking for has been helping us find Him. We are never alone in our search; He is with us every step of the way. But the search is not always an easy one.

Obstacles To Overcome

The journey of the Magi was a difficult one. They traveled a great distance, and in those days travel was slow, dangerous, grueling, and very costly. Furthermore, the sign in the heavens had not signified that they would *find* the king of the Jews, only that He had been born. The sign could not assure them that they would ever *see* this king, only that He existed. When they arrived in Jerusalem, their first question was "Where is the one who has been born king of the Jews?" (Matthew 2:2).

There was much uncertainty in their quest. There was danger on the road. And a myriad of other obstacles threatened the success of their journey.

Many today also face daunting obstacles in their search for the real Jesus. Religious obstacles, intellectual obstacles, relational obstacles, emotional obstacles, and spiritual obstacles. Some fear the unexpected. They aren't sure what Jesus might mean to their lives, to their own goals and ambitions. They may fear He will turn them into someone they don't want to become. Guilt over past sin or a present lifestyle can make others feel that Jesus would never *want* to find them, or they Him. Such formidable obstacles can make seekers wonder whether their search for Jesus could ever be successful.

Yet when the Magi had overcome all the obstacles, probably their greatest surprise was the joy they experienced. When the star stopped over Bethlehem, we are told, they were "overjoyed" (Matthew 2:10). Their search had ended, and they bowed down and worshiped the One they had sought. They may still have had many questions, but the most important one had been answered. Their quest was real; the sign was true. This miraculous child announced to them through a celestial anomaly had been found.

C. S. Lewis said that of all the emotions he expected to feel at his conversion, the one he was most surprised by, at finding Jesus, was joy. As Lewis writes, "Joy is the serious business of heaven."

To come to Christ is easy, because He wants us to come to Him (Matthew 11:28–30). But it is also hard, because our feelings, relationships, minds, and religious backgrounds can create real obstacles. Furthermore, we cannot hope to find Him without help.

Unwitting Helpers

The story makes it clear that while the Magi had seen His star, and come to worship Him, they didn't know exactly where to find Him. In fact, at a certain point the star they were following disappeared. Not until they left Herod and went on their way to Bethlehem did the star reappear to give them further guidance. God intervened at the beginning, showing them the star, and He intervened at the end of their journey to lead them directly to the place where the Christ child was.

The Magi were like so many who have a hint, a concept about God and Jesus; they are attracted to Him, but their knowledge is insufficient for them to come close and actually find Him. Without help they will never find Jesus. God needs to show them the way.

The wise men responded positively to the special celestial sign they had been given in their own country. But they did not initiate the search. God did. He sent the sign; they simply responded to it. Along with the star, God brought into their lives a jealous and tyrannical king with his own evil agenda, and a group of priests and teachers of the law who knew where the Christ was to be born but showed no interest in finding Him. Some situations and people that God brings into our lives to help us find Him are surprising—like the star, and the evil king, and the ambivalent religious leaders—but God uses them nonetheless. Many of them never even guess that God is using them in this manner, any more than Herod knew that God was using him to help the Magi.

God *wants* us to find Him, but He knows we can never accomplish this feat without His help. No wonder we are surprised to discover that we are not only the hunters, but the hunted.

Who Will We Find?

The Magi had not only found Jesus, they had also been *found* by Him. Who had set the star in the heavens for them to see? The baby before whom they bowed. There, before them, was the maker of all the stars and the heavens and the earth, who in a miracle of unprecedented proportion had taken the form of a tiny child, helpless, fragile, and vulnerable.

They had come to worship, but they had no idea who they had come to worship. And what they found must have astonished them. The star had foretold the birth of a king, but it had said nothing about a stable, or poverty, or humility. By the time the Magi arrived, Jesus and His parents were no longer in a stable (Matthew 2:11), but the story of His amazing birth surely must have been related to them.

These were important, learned, wealthy men from the East who had traveled a long distance at great personal cost—and what did they find? A mere child, born to a poor family in a tiny conquered country. Yet instead of turning away in disappointment or even anger at their discovery, the Magi rejoiced and worshiped.

Like the Magi, we may have some idea of what we will find when we go looking for Jesus, but it will always be inadequate. We will always be surprised! Surprised by wonder, surprised by joy, surprised by power clothed in humility.

From a human perspective, the Magi must have expected to find this baby king in a palace, surrounded by luxury, safety, and privilege. What they discovered instead left them only one response: joy and worship. It is the response of every single person who has ever found Jesus.

Whose Gift Was Greater?

At first glance it appears that the Magi were the most generous gift givers in the Christmas story. Yet the very opposite is true. Much has been made of their gifts of gold, frankincense, and myrrh, and over the years much meaning has been attached to each gift. These were, however, at that time, the typical gifts one would bring to a child of royal birth. The choice of gifts had been settled before they ever left their own country, before they ever found this amazing child.

So they presented their gifts. Then they worshiped.

The Magi had announced to Herod that they had come for this very purpose. They had come to worship and pay homage to a king. But this was no earthly king, and their worship must have been transformed as their hearts witnessed the scene before them. And their gifts paled.

Whatever we try to give to God, no matter how great, will always be less than what He gives us. The Magi had traveled far to see Him. Yet Jesus had traveled from heaven to find them. At great personal sacrifice they had made their journey. Yet how much more had Jesus sacrificed to leave His glory, His eternal dwelling place, and take upon Himself the nature of man, humbling Himself before His creation, just to greet them in that tiny house?

Their sacrifices, which must have seemed so great to them at the time, were infinitely smaller than the one He had already made to humble Himself before them. And they had no idea how much more He would sacrifice for them before His life was over.

We are accustomed to thinking that the greatest gift of the Magi was gold, frankincense, and myrrh. It wasn't. The greatest gift they brought was their devotion: their willingness to endure whatever it took and to look as long as it took to find what God had promised them through the sign. Their physical gifts paled in comparison.

To have seen the sign in the eastern sky and wondered about its meaning and import was one thing, but to undertake a difficult search to find this special person was quite another. They not only saw the sign — and surely they were not alone in seeing it—but they responded to it. As a result, they were rewarded with joy and the opportunity to worship at His feet.

Archbishop Fulton J. Sheen once wrote, "The simple shepherds heard the voice of an angel and found their Lamb; the wise men saw the light of a star and found their Wisdom."

What greater gift can we bring to Christ than our commitment to find Him no matter the cost, and when we have found Him, to worship Him?

The spirit of Christmas is found in those who see the sign and respond to it. They allow it to lead them to Him, even if the journey promises to be difficult. And whatever gift they would give to Him, they will find that what He gives them is infinitely greater.

To truly enter into the real spirit of Christmas also involves stepping outside our own worship and joy to help guide those still on the journey. Millions still seek Him, but they need help. We who have found Him—and been found by Him—are called to be their guides.

We must be patient with their questions, their doubts, and their confusion. Their journey is not an easy one, and they may run into many false guides—the Herods of this world—along the way. Our task is to encourage them, and maybe even to enlighten them with the knowledge that the One they seek is actually seeking them. That the hunters are also the hunted.

They need to know that this journey to Bethlehem, though difficult, is the most important thing they will ever do. And at journey's end they will find surprise, joy, and worship.

Reflection and Celebration

Every Christmas we encounter those who, while they are familiar with our cultural Christmas traditions, are still ignorant of their deeper meanings. Because of this, it is tempting to simply parrot or adorn ourselves with the familiar clichés: "Keep the Christ in Christmas," or "He is the Reason for the Season." Unfortunately, these sayings don't begin to explain the wonder of, or necessity of, the incarnation.

Instead of criticizing those who recognize only the cultural aspects of Christmas, why not ask God to help you gently and graciously share the true meaning of the incarnation with just one person this season. Ask Him to enable you to tell this person what the entrance of God into our world really means.

Instead of trying to find an opportunity to aggressively insert your views on Christmas into a discussion, why not begin asking some of your friends what Christmas really means to them? Don't criticize or judge their answers. Listen respectfully and patiently. You may learn something very important. Chances are extremely good that they will then ask you what you think.

If they do, speak graciously, humbly, and considerately. And perhaps this Christmas you will both be surprised by joy.

THIRTEEN

❄

The Keepers of Christmas

Christmas can come upon us with such a blinding fury and speed that we are left, after the celebration, out of breath and wondering what hit us. We're not sure if we had the Christmas spirit or not. But if we did, we're pretty sure it's gone now. We've "done" Christmas.

We're like the little girl who was so excited on Christmas Eve she could hardly contain herself. Her father was worried with bundles and burdens. Mom's nerves reached the breaking point more than once as she tried to make sure everything was cooked, wrapped, cleaned, and set. The little girl seemed to be in the way no matter where she went. Finally, she was hustled off to bed. As she knelt and said her bedtime prayers, the excitement and confusion of the day mixed her up a bit. As usual she ended her prayers with the Lord's Prayer, only this time she was heard to say, "Forgive us our Christmases, as we forgive those who Christmas against us."

Christmas often becomes an artificial spiritual stimulant. It's the one time of year when we find it easier to be a little more spiritual, a little less selfish. Many even think about God a little more. In Charles Dickens's

A Christmas Carol, Scrooge's good-hearted nephew, Fred, says to a grumpy Scrooge:

"I have always thought of Christmas time, when it has come round . . . as a good time: a kind, forgiving, charitable, pleasant time: the only time I know of, in the long calendar of the year, when men and women seem by one consent to open their shut-up hearts freely, and to think of people below them as if they really were fellow passengers to the grave, and not another race of creatures bound on other journeys. And therefore . . . though it has never put a scrap of gold or silver in my pockets, I believe that it has done me good, and will do me good; and I say, God bless it!"[1]

Many, like Fred, drink deeply of this spiritual stimulant at Christmas, but because they are unaccustomed to it, and when they realize that they no longer have their Christmas "fix," they enter the proverbial "spiritual morning after." So when the twenty-fifth comes and goes, they numbly start taking down the tree and putting away the decorations.

Post-Christmas letdown, Christmas hangover, call it what you like, but it is a very real experience for many. The Christmas stimulant was enjoyed, but now the false high brings us to a true low. Baby Jesus has been packed away along with the crèche until next year. The temporary anesthesia of excitement is gone, and now we have to face the grind of daily life again. But is the Christmas spirit something that is appropriate only for the Christmas season? Is there nothing to keep with us all year long?

Fortunately, there is, and evidence of it is found very close to the Christmas story in a mostly neglected period in baby Jesus' life. There, two characters emerge who, though usually not considered part of the traditional Christmas story, are very much a part of the real spirit of Christmas.

At this point in the story, Jesus was several months old. The star and the angels were gone, the shepherds and wise men had returned to their respective places and duties, and the manger was only a memory.

Despite the miraculous birth of God into our world, however, grimness and despair were still in great supply. But no matter how dark life may seem, no matter how horrible the situation may look, there are always those whose faith in God burns brightly. They are tiny candles fending off the encroaching darkness, stubbornly refusing to be extinguished.

Two such believers are found immediately following the traditional Christmas story. From the shepherds going back to their fields, "glorifying and praising God for all the things they had heard and seen" (Luke 2:20), we transition into "the rest of the story."

The Man with a Promise

About fifty days after Jesus' birth, Mary and Joseph fulfilled the Old Testament law of consecration, dedicating their firstborn son to the Lord (Exodus 13:2,12).

According to the law, Mary was ceremonially unclean until the fortieth day after she gave birth, whereupon she would offer a sacrifice and be restored to worship in the community. She could bring a year-old lamb for a burnt offering and a pair of young pigeons or turtledoves for a sin offering. If she was not able to bring a lamb, she could bring two young pigeons or two young turtledoves, one as a burnt offering and one as a sin offering. The priest would then make atonement for her and she would be purified (Leviticus 12:6–8).

Joseph and Mary were able to offer only the poorer sacrifice. But unbeknownst to them, there was someone at the temple eagerly awaiting the arrival of the one true sacrificial Lamb.

Strangely, most people don't associate Simeon with the traditional Christmas story. They stay for the manger, the star, the shepherds, and the wise men, then they turn the channel or close the book. To them, the Christmas story is over. Time to take down the tree, put away the lights, box up the decorations, and leave Christmas for another year.

But Luke tries to stop us. Before the story is ended we read, "Now there was a man in Jerusalem called Simeon" (Luke 2:25). It's almost as if Luke is saying, "Wait, don't leave yet. The story isn't over! There is something really important you don't want to miss."

Simeon had no impressive human résumé. He was not a prophet, priest, or king. But his heavenly résumé marks him as one of the most impressive of all biblical characters. He was, for all intents and purposes, what we call a layman. But of who else in Scripture, prior to the formation of the church, do we read, *"and the Holy Spirit was upon him"* (Luke 2:25)?

Keep in mind that the Holy Spirit had yet to indwell believers, as would happen at the Day of Pentecost, after

Jesus' resurrection. Only a few Old Testament saints had this blessing, and it was usually temporary. Yet Simeon enjoyed such a close and intimate walk with God that the Spirit of God revealed to him that before he died he would lay eyes on God's Messiah.

How long he had held onto that promise we do not know. Had it come when he was a young man, or when he was older? It seems likely, from Simeon's demeanor, that a lengthy period of time had elapsed between the giving of the promise and its fulfillment. How long had he been anxiously looking for the coming Messiah? How many days, months, years had he gone faithfully to the temple, expecting, hoping, to find the One promised to Israel?

Now, on the appointed day, Simeon, *"Moved by the Spirit ..."* went into the temple courts" (Luke 2:27, emphasis added). Did you catch that? Not in despair, not in doubt, not in frustration because the promise still wasn't fulfilled, but "moved by the Spirit." Simeon was righteous and devout, meaning he was in a right relationship with man and with God. His life was focused and faithful.

But would Simeon have been looking for a baby? There is no evidence to suggest this. In fact, a child was probably the least likely personage he was looking for. After all, the majority of Old Testament descriptions of Messiah speak of a mighty leader, a great warrior, a prince who would rule and conquer. Armed with that information and Simeon's promise, would you be checking all the baby strollers that went by? I wouldn't. I'd be looking for dynamic, imposing, leadership-type guys.

Simeon didn't know when he would see the Messiah. No time frame had been given him, except that it would be before he died, and he surely didn't know that day. So on this special morning when Simeon went to the temple with the Holy Spirit upon him, there is no indication it was because he knew he was going to discover the Christ child. Instead, it speaks of the fact that this was simply the way he lived.

This man walked with God, continually. While little note was taken of him on earth, he was a big man in heaven. No one else had received this promise. And in God's sovereign plan, He directed that Simeon and Joseph and Mary would be at the temple at the same place, at the same time. And that somehow Simeon would clearly recognize that this common couple held in their arms the hope of Israel, the salvation of God, the light of revelation to the Gentiles, the glory of Israel.

The moment Simeon saw them, he must have known. How? We can't guess. But I picture him walking over to Mary and Joseph and suddenly realizing that his prayers had finally been answered. Can you imagine the look on his face as he suddenly knew, beyond a shadow of a doubt, that this baby was the fulfillment of his personal promise and God's promise to the world?

I envision tears in his eyes as he asks to hold the child, and as the teenage mother hands her son to this man of God. And with Jesus, his Redeemer, his own Messiah in his arms, Simeon's joy overflowed and he "took him in his arms and praised God, saying: 'Sovereign Lord, as you have promised, you now dismiss your servant in peace. For my eyes have seen your salvation, which you have prepared in the sight of all people, a light for revelation to the Gentiles and for glory to your people Israel'" (Luke 2:28–32).

The Woman with a Purpose

efore Mary and Joseph's amazement at this reaction to their son has a chance to subside an old woman standing nearby approaches them.

"There was also a prophetess, Anna, the daughter of Phanuel, of the tribe of Asher. She was very old; she had lived with her husband seven years after her marriage, and then was a widow until she was eighty-four. She never left the temple but worshiped night and day, fasting and praying. Coming up to them at that very moment, she gave thanks to God and spoke about the child to all who were looking forward to the redemption of Jerusalem" (Luke 2:36–38).

Anna is old, and her physical eyes are dim, her body frail, her walk slow and labored. Yet she instantly recognizes God's promised One. She hurries over to look upon the child and begins pouring out lavish praise to God, announcing to all within earshot that the redemption of Israel, the promised Messiah, has come.

Anna apparently had not been given the kind of vision that Simeon had, and it may even have been this particular event in her life that set her apart as a prophetess. Whatever the case, she had demonstrated her devotion to the Lord for years. In waiting for Messiah, she had fasted and prayed, never leaving the temple.

I love Anna. She wasn't a queen, or a woman of great renown. She had been a widow for many years, and if she had children, we don't hear of them. She seems to be one of those faithful souls who have known the pain of life and death. Yet did she become bitter and cynical about life and God? No. Instead, she devoted her entire life to serving Him.

Imagine her joy as she looks down and beholds her promised Messiah. What hope must have filled her soul! And what joy that she has been given the privilege of proclaiming His arrival.

The Keepers of Christmas

*I*s the spirit of Christmas seasonal? Simeon and Anna show us that it is not. The true keepers of Christmas are those who, when the holiday excitement is over, remain just as firmly committed to the joy of the risen Messiah as ever. They wait patiently, oh so patiently, for the promises of God to be fulfilled in their lives.

Spiritual passion is not a once-a-year event for them, so they suffer no spiritual hangovers. Like Simeon and Anna, who waited so patiently for Messiah to come, they wait with the same patience for Him to come back. For them, Christmas is never over, the celebration never ends, and the wonder never wears off. Like Anna, they celebrate Christmas by speaking to all who are looking for redemption, all who are in need of a Savior. These keepers of Christmas continue to faithfully point out the light of revelation to the Gentiles, and the Glory of Israel. Nothing is over for them. On the contrary, everything is just beginning.

Of all the famous, important, and powerful people who lived in Jesus' day, most have passed from history, never to be remembered. Yet for thousands of years, the testimony and faithfulness of Simeon and Anna have lived on. Brighter lights have flamed and burned out. Yet these faithful burn more brightly than ever.

So before you dismantle the tree, pack away the decorations, and close the chapter on this year's Christmas story, think about how you will keep the Christmas flame burning bright all year long.

Ask God to remind you of the lives of Simeon and Anna. Remember these simple folks who were entrusted with a divine message—a message that must not be packed away until next year, but proclaimed now and tomorrow and forever.

Who are the keepers of Christmas? We are. Let us keep it well.

Reflection and Celebration

We have all heard the stories of those who love Christmas so much that they never take down their decorations or lights. Perhaps we even know some of these folks. They watch Christmas movies and play their Christmas music all year long. They have become so attached to the cultural message and images of Christmas that they are simply unwilling to leave Christmas to go back to "normal life."

While this may strike us as strange or weird or even funny, I would suggest we join them. Not in keeping our Christmas decorations up all year round, for that is not the true source of our Christmas joy, but in being keepers of the spirit of Christmas.

What virtues or activities do you tend to "put away" every Christmas? Should these truly be seasonal? Have you ever noticed that you become a different (better) person at Christmas? Do we really want to pack up our joy and anticipation and put it away for another year?

Take time this Christmas and examine those virtues (joy, hope, compassion, generosity, patience, love) that tend to be stronger in you at Christmas. Write them down. Then ask God to help you carry these virtues over into January, then February, and longer, until they become permanent residents of your character.

Also, think about the testimonies of Simeon and Anna. If it is important that we consider Jesus' true purpose and identity in December, is it any less important for us to consider them in January, or July, or October? Become a keeper of Christmas — and keep it all year long.

Perhaps you could take a small Christmas ornament, such as a manger or an angel, and place it in different places around your home each month of the year. Each time you see the ornament, remind yourself that you are a "Keeper of Christmas" and ask God for help in keeping the light of anticipation and expectation of His coming again burning brightly in your heart.

FOURTEEN

❋

The Last Christmas Morning

I love Christmas and all it represents. I have since I was a little boy. And the week following Christmas I invariably experience a sad nostalgia for the passing of the season. Partly because I am hopelessly sentimental, and partly because, frankly, I miss the anticipation, the joy, the warmth, and the hope of the season. For one brief shining moment in my year, the world seems to change a little for the better. I seem to change a little for the better.

Each year after Thanksgiving our kids begin begging us to get out our Christmas decorations and put up the lights. So one day, as is our tradition, we put on our Christmas CDs, open up the boxes of ornaments and decorations, and with each piece we unpack we are reminded of Christmases past. Each ornament has a story and a history to it, and our kids enjoy hanging them on the tree and placing the decorations around our house.

But when it is time to put everything away in the boxes and bins after Christmas, they are not nearly so eager. Preparing for the season is exciting, but parting from it is like saying goodbye to beloved family and friends when they leave after the holidays. We have just had a wonderful experience, and we don't want it to end. The days and weeks following Christmas slowly steal the wonder of those holy days, and as we look around at a house that now looks strangely bare, we can't help thinking: Wouldn't it be great if Christmas could last forever?

But this is not just about decorations and warm family gatherings. You see, at Christmas we get a taste of the eternal, and it whets our appetite for more. At Christmas, strained relationships often seem better as we are more willing to put aside our differences. Our three children suddenly forget to bicker and complain about each other and begin asking what the others want for Christmas. Giving takes precedence over getting. The Schaeffer household experiences holiness, peace, joy, generosity, and love in ways we don't at other times, and our souls long for more.

Then the season ends, and the grudge we overlooked during Christmas flares up again after the new year. The weaknesses in others we were more willing to overlook during the holiday season become unacceptable once more. Our patience, strengthened and encouraged by the season, grows short again. Peace with God is a reality to those who have placed their faith in Him, but perfect peace with each other is still unattainable.

Though many promises of the Bible have been fulfilled — the Messiah has come, and our salvation has been secured — the needles of the tree of life still fall from the branches, just like the dead needles fall from our lifeless Christmas tree at a touch. Pain, disappointment, sorrow, and trials, which can be anesthetized by the Christmas season, soon reappear. Life on planet Earth is still the same.

Life After Christmas

*W*hen I observe our own post-Christmas letdown, I can't help but wonder what life was like for Mary and Joseph and the other characters in the Christmas story a year later? The shepherds were back in the fields with the sheep. Had they been changed? Inevitably. But had life itself changed that much for them? Probably not. Did they ever wish they could recapture the surprise, joy, and holiness of that angelic visitation and that holy moment at the manger? Did they wish those blessed moments could have lasted longer?

I wonder whether those shepherds watched the sky expectantly for the rest of their lives. Would the angels re-appear? Would they bring another glorious message? Were the shepherds' dreams filled with memories of that angelic visitation?

The Magi returned to their own homeland and their old lives. Life must go on, even after you've witnessed a miracle. The star that had guided them had disappeared from the sky, and their lives had been forever changed, but life on earth had not. Would they, like the shepherds, be looking for a repeat of the miracle? Would there be another celestial sign? Did they spend the rest of their lives trying to fully understand the miracle they had witnessed? Or did the daily grind of life slowly shift their focus away from that miraculous time?

Herod, the ruthless genocidal monarch, continued to abuse his power to secure his kingdom against all challengers. But did he ever find peace of mind regarding "the child born king of the Jews," or did he remain troubled? Did he worry that somehow this renegade child-king had escaped his deadly purge and might threaten his rule one day? Did the Scriptures that the chief priests and scribes had shared with him haunt his dreams?

For a time, Mary and Joseph had to live in Egypt as refugees, hiding their son from the murderous plot of Herod. Eventually, though, they returned to their home in Nazareth—Joseph to his carpentry shop and Mary to her life of homemaking and mothering. They would never be the same as a result of their experiences, but life, with its hardship and pain, daily routine, and, yes, joy and success would go on.

Yet despite this return to the ordinary sameness of life, in reality, nothing would ever be the same again.

The Invisible Change

Everything changed when Jesus entered our world. The power of sin would soon be broken, and Satan's plans would be crushed. God's grace had been born into our world—a power so great nothing could prevail against it. The spiritual axis of the world had shifted violently, and the effect could not have been more profound if the earth's physical axis had shifted.

Today, the sinful momentum of our world continues, making everything seem as it was before Jesus came. But a new kingdom has been established. And by faith we live in the long shadow of that promise. At Christmas the shadow seems to lift for a moment and we seem so much closer to that day. With its celebration, joy, excitement, warmth, and holiness Christmas reminds us that although many wonderful promises have been fulfilled in our midst, we are still waiting for the last, eternal, Christmas morning — the one that will last forever.

As J. B. Phillips wrote, "Nothing can alter the fact that we live on a visited planet." And he urges us as we daily tread the surface of this planet to "reflect with confidence that 'my God has been here, here on this planet!'"[1] Have you ever taken that into account during your celebration of this holy event? *Your God walked this earth.* He fingered the leaves on the trees and quenched His parched throat with cool water. He watched the sun rise and set, and followed the moon across the night sky.

Phillips goes on to write, "When God decides that the human experiment has gone on long enough, yes, even in the midst of what appears to be confusion and incompleteness, Christ will come again! This is what the New Testament teaches. This is the message of Advent. It is for us to be alert, vigilant and industrious, so that His coming will not be a terror but an overwhelming act of joy."[2]

Perhaps that is one of the elements that make our celebrations bittersweet. A part of us wants to hold on to the hope of a better world, a world where Christ has come to stay, where sin will be banished from our hearts as well as our world. We desperately want to embrace all that Christmas promises, especially Immanuel—God with us. He came to live with us, and now within us, but His inner presence only makes us desire more. The Savior has come and opened our eyes to perfect eternity, and we can't help experiencing a sort of heavenly homesickness.

We who wait for the promise must wait a bit longer, and waiting is difficult. "For many people, waiting is an awful desert between where they are and where they want to go," writes Henri Nouwen. "And people do not like such a place. They want to get out of it by doing something.... It impresses me, therefore, that all the figures who appear on the first pages of Luke's gospel are waiting. Zechariah and Elizabeth are waiting. Mary is waiting. Simeon and Anna, who were at the temple when Jesus was brought in, were waiting. The whole opening scene of the good news is filled with waiting people ... People who wait have received a promise that allows them to wait. They have received something that is at work in them, like a seed that has started to grow. This is very important. We can only really wait if what we are waiting for has already begun for us. So waiting is never a movement from nothing to something. It is always a movement from something to something more."[3]

Christmas provides a looking glass for all believers. God came to live among us, and now we wait for the day when we will live with Him forever. Life as we know it is not life as it will always be. As surely as God kept His promise to enter our world and bring us back to Him, so He will take us to be with Him one day. We long to live in His perfect presence as naturally as we live in this fallen, sad, and dying world.

The blessed hope and the painful reality are rarely in greater contrast than at Christmas. Our greatest dreams and our deepest despair often intersect in the holy season. Both are real — hence our conflict. The celebration of Christmas is a delicious spiritual hors d'oeuvre to eternity, tantalizing us with reminders that the banquet is yet to come, and it will be eternally satisfying.

Keeping the Lights On

art of the real Christmas spirit is the hope it inspires in us of the day when Jesus will come again, no longer the baby in the manger, but the Lord of all the earth. That is the ultimate fulfillment of all that Christmas promises. The Babe from Bethlehem will revisit the planet He once called home. But this time He will not come in humility; He will come in power. Death will be overcome forever, replaced by eternal life. Old things will pass away; behold, new things will come.

Lies will be replaced with truth, and injustice will become extinct. Sadness, pain, regret, loss, failure, and tears will pass away like the ice age, never to return. And those of us who spent so many years celebrating Christmas in the firm belief that one day faith would become sight will wake to that eternal morning. Until then, in each celebration of Christmas we are turning the light on in anticipation of that final morning.

Pastor and author Robert Russell tells the story of a family in their subdivision that kept their Christmas lights on long after the season was past. In fact, they were still on through January and the first of February. As the middle of February drew near, Russell couldn't help being a little critical. *If I were too lazy to take my Christmas lights down, I think I'd at least turn them off at night*, he thought. But about the middle of March a sign appeared outside the house that explained why they'd left the lights on. It said simply, "Welcome home, Jimmy." Russell then learned that the family had a son in Vietnam, and they had unashamedly left their Christmas lights on in anticipation of his return.

Lights are a symbol of hope. And Christmas is how we "keep the lights on" anticipating His return.[4]

All the joys of all our Christmas experiences will pale before the advent of the last, eternal, Christmas morning. The divine Christmas Light will never be extinguished, the joy will never fade, the hope will finally be fulfilled. The King—our King—will have come at last. The long promised kingdom of God will be ushered in, and our fervent dreams will be reality.

Peace on earth, good will to men will no longer be a hope or a motto on a Christmas card. It will be the actual inheritance of all who have longed for His appearing. Each Christmas we keep the lights on, knowing that promise is a little closer.

When we speak of the hope of Christmas, we are imagining something other than what we are currently experiencing—something better, something eternal.

Imagine the last Christmas morning. Imagine what life will be like when our world is ruled by our Lord who loved us so much that He died for us. What will life be like when the only emotions that fill our hearts are joy and love and peace? What will it be like to have no fear, no anxiety, no anger, no envy, no jealousy, no tears or sadness, because the world in which we live is so perfect that no such emotions can be produced? What will it be like to be so changed internally that we actually fit in a perfect world, so changed that we have become something fundamentally different than we can ever hope to attain here on earth? What will it be like to live a perfect life—forever? What eternal wonders await those who will walk and live forever with our God in His perfect world?

Through His first coming—what we call Christmas— God revealed to us how much we have to look forward to in His Second Coming. And with every Christmas morning I experience, I know I am that much closer to the last Christmas morning.

So this Christmas, and for all the days thereafter, my goal is to keep the lights on in my heart in anticipation of His return. When He does, the last Christmas morning will dawn—and never end.

Reflection and Celebration

During the Christmas season, reflection is one of the most precious gifts we can give ourselves. Too often, with all our busyness and preparations, we allow precious little time to quietly contemplate all the season promises. Reflection at warp speed is impossible, so decide this year to make a change.

This year, allow yourself—even schedule yourself—a quiet walk. Find a place where you can see more of what God has made than what man has made. A park, a country road, or just a quiet spot where you can sit and think, or walk and ponder. As you do, remind yourself: *My God walked this planet*. Look at the trees, the sky, the mountains, the stars, the moon. Remember that Jesus saw these too. You live on a visited planet.

Then let your thoughts drift forward, into the future, to when He comes again. Allow all the pain and sorrows and difficulties you face today to be put in this eternal perspective. A day is coming, as surely as the first Christmas morning, when He will reappear and the last Christmas morning will begin and never end. The true joy of Christmas does not require change in our earthly circumstances, only our earthly perspective.

In heaven the plans are ready. And one day earth will not only be revisited, it will be renewed, and so will we. He will come again and you will see Him, face to face, forever. Allow yourself to indulge in some pre-arrival celebration. If you can manage to do this, your Christmas will be a true celebration.

FIFTEEN

❄

We Call It
Christmas

We call it Christmas. The incarnation. The day God became a man. But have you ever noticed that our view of that amazing event is always vertical? We are focused, as we should be, on God coming down to us — or, perhaps more accurately, God appearing among us.

This is the scene we are allowed to see. And it is amazing. So amazing that it will take forever to truly grasp it. Yet there is another scene, one we have not been able to see. One we can only imagine. And that is what I'd like for you to do with me for a few moments. Imagine the incredible moment when Jesus left His proper place in heaven. A place known only to Him, where His glory dwells in unapproachable light. Have you ever wondered about that moment?

Author Madeleine L'Engle brings us a sense of this moment when she writes, "Was there a moment, known only to God, when all the stars held their breath, when the galaxies paused in their dance for a fraction of a second, and the Word, who had called it all into being, went with all His love into the womb of a young girl, and the universe started to breathe again, and the ancient harmonies resumed their song, and the angels clapped their hands for joy?"[1]

In the past, we were allowed to see visible manifestations of His Shekinah glory. We saw the cloud by day, the fire by night, the burning bush, the earthquake, the great wind. These were not God. They were not even His shadow. They were the leaves that the power of the passing wind blows off the trees, evidence of His presence presented for those with weak eyes and weaker faith. We saw but an eclipse of His glory, and only indirectly, for our fragile senses were not equipped to look upon or fathom such glory.

But there is another scene we have never really been told much about. It is, in fact, mentioned only in passing when we are told that He "who being in very nature God … made Himself nothing" (Philippians 2:6–7).

Nothing? How could God make Himself nothing? Only by comparing His eternal glory, which our world cannot contain, with the feeble human nature that He would take upon Himself. There was simply "nothing" in that human nature or tiny body that our God took upon Himself that compared with His prior glory.

He *made* Himself nothing. Suddenly His creative power was called upon again, creating a new form for His eternal existence. But instead of creating everything out of nothing, He who holds all things together would now pour everything into nothing.

With every inch He descended to earth, He allowed His glory to leak away, until His arrival on earth found Him empty. Only heaven would remember His former glory.

Changes in Heaven

At a specific moment, if we can call it that, every-thing in heaven that had remained the same for eternity past *changed*. A decision made in eternity past, in the eternal perfect mind of God, suddenly reached that holy moment for which it had been born. The Son left the side of the Father and became a man.

We know what happened on earth after that, but what about heaven? What was the reaction of the Father as His Son voluntarily undertook this suicide rescue mission? What emotions passed between the Father and the Son? What did the Son feel as the time drew near to leave His glory and His Father's side and to take on a human nature?

In some way deeper than the mysteries of the universe, their relationship would be different. And in at least one way, the Son would never be the same, for He had added human nature to His eternal being. Now eternal glory would emanate forever from One we could see, from One we could touch, from One who had touched us, and who could now touch us forever. This is the very least of what Paul meant when he told the Philippians that "he humbled himself" (Philippians 2:8). Any human words fail to adequately describe that truth.

Was there silence in heaven when the Son left His glory? Did the solemnity of the moment and the eternal ramifica-tions cause a hush? Did all heaven mourn His departure, even while angels sang His praises on earth? Or was there confident praise and adoration among the host of heaven and the Godhead? Knowing that the salvation of mankind was imminent, did His departure elicit the same praise and exaltation that visited the shepherds only moments later?

What was the mood in heaven? Would the knowledge that death could not hold Him, or the joy of the salvation that He would provide, overrule the pain of the separation?

Human wisdom has no answer. All we can do is conjecture. That is what author J. B. Phillips did when he "imagined" what the entire incarnation must have been like from the perspective of the angels. Just for a few moments, imagine along with him, and see where it takes you.

The Angels' Point of View

Once upon a time a very young angel was being shown round the splendors and glories of the universes by a senior and experienced angel. To tell the truth, the little angel was beginning to be tired and a little bored. He had been shown whirling galaxies and blazing suns, infinite distances in the deathly cold of interstellar space, and to his mind there seemed to be an awful lot of it all. Finally he was shown the galaxy of which our planetary system is but a small part. As the two of them drew near to the star which we call our sun and to its circling planets, the senior angel pointed to a small and rather insignificant sphere turning very slowly on its axis. It looked as dull as a dirty tennis ball to the little angel whose mind was filled with the size and glory of what he had seen.

"I want you to watch that one particularly," said the senior angel, pointing with his finger.

"Well, it looks very small and rather dirty to me," said the little angel. "What's special about that one?"

"That," replied his senior solemnly, "is the Visited Planet."

"Visited?" said the little one. "You don't mean visited by—"

"Indeed I do. That ball, which I have no doubt looks to you small and insignificant and not perhaps overclean, has been visited by our young Prince of Glory." And at these words he bowed his head reverently.

"But how?" queried the younger one. "Do you mean that our great and glorious Prince, with all these wonders and splendors of His Creation, and millions more that I'm sure I haven't seen yet, went down in Person to this fifth-rate little ball? Why should He do a thing like that?"

"It isn't for us," said his senior, a little stiffly, "to question His 'why's,' except that I must point out to you that He is not impressed by size and numbers as you seem to be. But that He really went I know, and all of us in Heaven who know anything know that. As to why He became one of them... How else do you suppose could He visit them?"

The little angel's face wrinkled in disgust.

"Do you mean to tell me," he said, "that He stooped so low as to become one of those creeping, crawling creatures of that floating ball?"

"I do, and I don't think He would like you to call them 'creeping crawling creatures' in that tone of voice. For, strange as it may seem to us, He loves them. He went down to visit them to lift them up to become like Him."

The little angel looked blank. Such a thought was almost beyond his comprehension.

"Close your eyes for a moment," said the senior angel, "and we will go back in what they call Time."

While the little angel's eyes were closed and the two of them moved nearer to the spinning ball, it stopped its spinning, spun backward quite fast for a while, and then slowly resumed its usual rotation.

"Now look!" and as the little angel did as he was told, there appeared here and there on the dull surface of the globe little flashes of light, some merely momentary and some persisting for quite a time.

"Well, what am I seeing now?" queried the little angel.

"You are watching this little world as it was some thousands of years ago," returned his companion. "Every flash and glow of light that you see is something of the Father's knowledge and wisdom breaking into the minds and hearts of people who live upon the earth. Not many people, you see, can hear His Voice or understand what He says, even though He is speaking gently and quietly to them all the time."

"Why are they so blind and deaf and stupid?" asked the junior angel rather crossly.

"It is not for us to judge them. We who live in the Splendor have no idea what it is like to live in the dark. We hear the music and the Voice like the sound of many waters every day of our lives, but to them—well, there is much darkness and much noise and much distraction upon the earth. Only a few who are quiet and humble and wise hear His voice. But watch, for in a moment you will see something truly wonderful."

The Earth went on turning and circling round the sun, and then, quite suddenly, in the upper half of the globe there appeared a light, tiny, but so bright in its intensity that both the angels hid their eyes.

"I think I can guess," said the little angel in a low voice. "That was the Visit, wasn't it?"

"Yes, that was the Visit. The Light Himself went down there and lived among them; but in a moment, and you will be able to tell that even with your eyes closed, the light will go out."

"But why? Could He not bear their darkness and stupidity? Did He have to return here?"

"No, it wasn't that," returned the senior angel. His voice was stern and sad. "They failed to recognize Him for Who He was—or at least only a handful knew Him. For the most part they preferred their darkness to His Light, and in the end they killed Him."

"The fools, the crazy fools! They don't deserve—"

"Neither you nor I nor any other angel knows why they were so foolish and so wicked. Nor can we say what they deserve or don't deserve. But the fact remains, they killed our Prince of Glory while He was Man amongst them."

"And that, I suppose, was the end? I see the whole Earth has gone black and dark. All right, I won't judge them, but surely that is all they could expect?"

"Wait. We are still far from the end of the story of the Visited Planet. Watch now, but be ready to cover your eyes again."

In utter blackness the Earth turned round three times, and then there blazed with unbearable radiance a point of light.

"What now?" asked the little angel shielding his eyes.

"They killed Him, all right, but He conquered death. The thing most of them dread and fear all their lives He broke and conquered. He rose again, and a few of them saw Him, and from then on became His utterly devoted slaves."

"Thank God for that!" said the little angel.

"Amen. Open your eyes now; the dazzling light has gone. The Prince has returned to His Home of Light. But watch the Earth now."

As they looked, in place of the dazzling light there was a bright glow which throbbed and pulsated. And then as the Earth turned many times, little points of light spread out. A few flickered and died, but for the most part the lights burned steadily, and as they continued to watch, in many parts of the globe there was a glow over many areas.

"You see what is happening?" asked the senior angel. "The bright glow is the company of loyal men and women He left behind, and with His help they spread the glow, and now lights begin to shine all over the Earth."

"Yes, yes," said the little angel impatiently. "But how does it end? Will the little lights join up with one another? Will it all be light, as it is in Heaven?"

His senior shook his head. "We simply do not know," he replied. "It is in the Father's hands. Sometimes it is agony to watch, and sometimes it is joy unspeakable. The end is not yet. But now I am sure you can see why this little ball is so important. He has visited it; He is working out His Plan upon it."

"Yes, I see, though I don't understand. I shall never forget that this is the Visited Planet."[2]

The Heavenly Audience

*T*hough Phillips's story is fanciful, it reminds us that heaven too was an audience to Christmas. Our Lord did indeed leave His glory and the company of the angels. He did it to show us what could not be shown from heaven — the great extent of His love. We would have to see it up close.

When adults want to speak to a small child gently and effectively, they bend down and accommodate themselves to the child's size and understanding. In the same way, the Lord of heaven voluntarily accommodated Himself to us in the incarnation. He made Himself like us in form so that we might become like Him in holiness.

The incarnation, as we call it, mixes pain and sorrow so perfectly with hope and joy that we cannot know what transpired in heaven before our Lord left His heavenly tarmac. Our perspective will, I fear, always be skewed. The moment was too glorious to truly understand. We will always see Christmas from this side, at least as long as we are on this side.

Today we call it Christmas. Only eternity knows what we shall call it forever.

The Real Spirit of Christmas

*A*nd so we finally find ourselves, once again, in the place we began: in search of something we might have once thought impossible to truly discover.

We have examined the story of the first Christmas, the characters and their reactions, and we have examined our own reactions to the story. In all these things we have been searching, again and again, for the real spirit of Christmas. What is it and can it really be found? Can I know for sure that I have it?

The answer to these questions is a profound "Yes!" For when all is said and done, and all the events of the story are considered, I believe the Christmas spirit is not as elusive as we might have imagined. And I can say with some certainty what the *real* spirit of Christmas is.

The real Christmas spirit is a deep-seated, lingering joy in knowing that the story is *true*!

Remove the trees, and the lights, and the poinsettias, and the candles, and the decorations, and the presents, and the food, and the music . . . and the story is still there. It is still true and our joy is still full!

The search is over. Let the rejoicing begin!

Reflection and Celebration

The story is true! Let that thought slowly simmer in you.

How does this simple thought transform your present circumstances? The story of your life is inexorably mixed in with this truth: you have a Savior who is Christ the Lord! Your life, indeed all heaven and earth, has been changed because of this marvelous truth. Present difficulties cannot erase the truth, pain cannot remove its reality, loss cannot usurp the joy of this event and its implications. They are, in fact, the reason we can rejoice so greatly. This life with all its attending difficulty is making way for a new, better one. All because the story is true!

Are you looking for a new and more meaningful way to celebrate the incarnation with your family, friends, or other Christians? This year, after the Christmas carols and the reading of the story from the Gospels, try something that is certain to get everyone thinking deeper about His birth and what it means.

After you have served the hot chocolate or cider, have someone read J. B. Phillips's story, "The Angels' Point of View." When the story is finished, ask everyone to write down what new thought or perspective they gained through this story. Then have them fold up their paper and place it in a large bowl or basket. During the rest of your time together, take turns reaching into the bowl and reading someone's thoughts. This will likely spur some great discussions and focus everyone on the incredible event we call Christmas.

Notes

Chapter One: What Is the Christmas Spirit Anyway?

[1] Bill Johnson, "A Lesson in Catching the Christmas Spirit," *Orange County Register*.

Chapter Three: We're No Longer Home Alone

[1] Leith Anderson, "A God's-Eye View of Christmas," *Preaching Today* 208.

[2] Dietrich Bonhoeffer, "The Coming of Jesus in Our Midst," in *A Testament to Freedom, The Essential Writings of Dietrich Bonhoeffer*, edited by Geoffrey B. Kelly and F. Burton Nelson (San Francisco: Harper San Francisco, 1995).

Chapter Four: For All the People

[1] "To Illustrate Plus," *Leadership Journal* (Spring 1999): 75.

Chapter Six: The God We Thought We Knew

[1] Philip Yancey, *The Jesus I Never Knew* (Grand Rapids: Zondervan, 1995), 36–37.

[2] J. B. Phillips, "The Christian Year," in *Good News: Thoughts on God and Man* (New York: Macmillan, 1963).

Chapter Seven: Givers or Receivers?

[1] William Willimon, "The God We Hardly Knew," *Christian Century* (December 21–28, 1988).

Chapter Eight: Beware the Christmas Grinches!

[1] Upton Sinclair in *Draper's Book of Quotations for the Christian World*, compiled by Edythe Draper (Wheaton, Ill.: Tyndale House Publishers, 1992), #1370.

[2] Dietrich Bonhoeffer, "The Coming of Jesus in Our Midst," in *A*

Testament to Freedom, The Essential Writings of Dietrich Bonhoeffer, edited by Geoffrey B. Kelly and F. Burton Nelson (San Francisco: Harper San Francisco, 1995).

[3] Ravi Zacharias, "Questions I Would Like To Ask God," *Just Thinking* (Winter 1998).

[4] Reynolds Price, "Jesus of Nazareth: Then and Now," *Time* (December, 6, 1999): 86.

[5] H.G. Wells. Source unknown.

[6] Martin Luther, "Sermon for Christmas Day: Luke 2:1–14" (1521–22) in *The Sermons of Martin Luther* (Minneapolis: Lutherans in All Lands Press, 1906).

Chapter Nine: The March of the Once-Wooden Soldiers

[1] Madeleine L'Engle, *Bright Evening Star* (Crosswicks, Inc., 1997).

Chapter Ten: One More Life To Give

[1] Steve Brown, *Overcoming Setbacks* (Colorado Springs: Navpress, 1992), 179–180.

[2] Vance Havner in *Draper's Book of Quotations for the Christian World*, compiled by Edythe Draper (Wheaton, Ill.: Tyndale House Publishers, 1992), #1360.

Chapter Eleven: When It Doesn't Feel Like Christmas

[1] Adapted from Dr. Thomas Tewell, *The Communicator's Companion* (March 21, 2002).

[2] Brennan Manning, "The Shipwrecked at the Stable," *Lion and Lamb: The Relentless Tenderness of Jesus*, (Grand Rapids: Chosen Books, a division of Baker Book House, 1986).

[3] Jill Briscoe, "Keeping the Adventure in Ministry," *Leadership Journal* (Summer 1996).

[4] Emmy Arnold, "Christmas Joy," *When the Time Was Fulfilled* (Farmington, Pa.: Plough, 1965).

Chapter Twelve: The Magi's Surprise

[1] Carol McGraw, "Who Say Ye That I Am?" *Orange County Register* 25 December 1995, sec. Religion.

Chapter Thirteen: The Keepers of Christmas

[1] Charles Dickens, *A Christmas Carol,* in *Illustrations Unlimited,* edited by James S. Hewitt (Wheaton, Ill.: Tyndale House Publishers, 1988), 77.

Chapter Fourteen: The Last Christmas Morning

[1] J. B. Phillips, "The Christian Year," *Good News: Thoughts on God and Man* (New York: Macmillan, 1963).
[2] Ibid.
[3] Henri J. M. Nouwen, "A Spirituality of Waiting" in *The Upper Weavings Reader,* edited by John S. Magabgab (Nashville: The Upper Room, 1993).
[4] Robert Russell, author and pastor of Southeast Christian Church, Louisville, Kentucky, in his sermon "Jesus Came To Be the Light," Preaching Today audio #195.

Chapter Fifteen: We Call It Christmas

[1] Madeleine L'Engle, *Bright Evening Star,* (Crosswicks, Inc., 1997).
[2] J. B. Phillips, "The Angels' Point of View," *New Testament Christianity* (New York: Macmillan, 1956), 15–19.

Note to the Reader

The publisher invites you to share your response to the message of this book by writing Discovery House Publishers, Box 3566, Grand Rapids, MI 49501, USA. For information about other Discovery House books, music, or videos, contact us at the same address or call 1-800-653-8333. Find us on the Internet at http://www.dhp.org/ or send e-mail to books@dhp.org.

About the Author

*D*an *Schaeffer* has been a pastor for twenty years in Southern California. He is a graduate of Grace Bible Institute in Long Beach and Talbot School of Theology (Biola University). An award-winning writer, Dan's articles have appeared in *Reader's Digest*, *A 3rd Serving of Chicken Soup for the Soul*, and a *Reader's Digest* anthology. He is the author of five books, including *When Faith and Decisions Collide* and *Defining Moments*, and has updated and edited a Christian classic written by William Nicholson, *The Six Miracles of Calvary*. Dan co-pastors Shoreline Community Church in Santa Barbara, California. You can find out more about Dan and his work at his Web site: www.danschaeffer.com.